The Top Ninja Dual Zone Air Fryer Cookbook 2023

1001 Days Effortless and Flavorful Ninja Foodi Air Fryer Meals You Will Love to Fry, Roast, Grill and Bake Using UK Measurements

Anne R. Rael

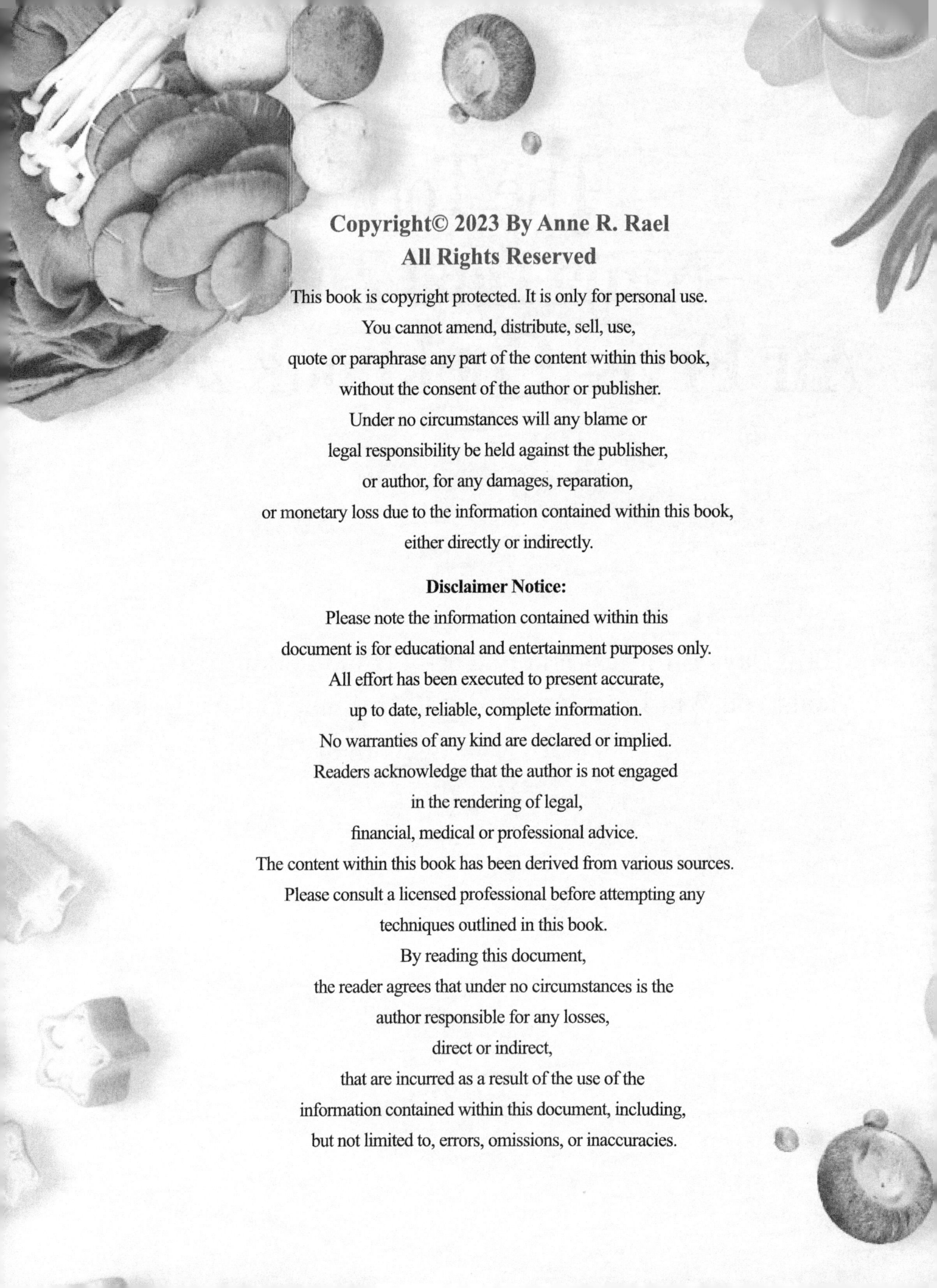

Copyright© 2023 By Anne R. Rael
All Rights Reserved

This book is copyright protected. It is only for personal use.
You cannot amend, distribute, sell, use,
quote or paraphrase any part of the content within this book,
without the consent of the author or publisher.
Under no circumstances will any blame or
legal responsibility be held against the publisher,
or author, for any damages, reparation,
or monetary loss due to the information contained within this book,
either directly or indirectly.

Disclaimer Notice:

Please note the information contained within this
document is for educational and entertainment purposes only.
All effort has been executed to present accurate,
up to date, reliable, complete information.
No warranties of any kind are declared or implied.
Readers acknowledge that the author is not engaged
in the rendering of legal,
financial, medical or professional advice.
The content within this book has been derived from various sources.
Please consult a licensed professional before attempting any
techniques outlined in this book.
By reading this document,
the reader agrees that under no circumstances is the
author responsible for any losses,
direct or indirect,
that are incurred as a result of the use of the
information contained within this document, including,
but not limited to, errors, omissions, or inaccuracies.

Contents

Introduction 1
- Getting to know the Ninja Dual Zone......... 1
- So, What is the Ninja Dual Zone Air Fryer? 2
- Why Choose the Ninja Dual Zone? 2
- The Benefits of the Ninja Dual Zone Air Fryer 2
- How to Clean the Ninja Dual Zone Air Fryer? 3
- Possible Risks 3
- Tips and Tricks to Using the Ninja Dual Zone Air Fryer 4
- FAQs 5

Chapter 1: Breakfast Recipes 6
- Churro Waffles 6
- Breakfast Pita 6
- Monte Cristo Sandwich 7
- Corn Fritters 7
- Shakshuka 8
- Breakfast Egg Rolls 8
- Bacon and Egg Breakfast Pockets 9
- French Toast Sticks 9
- Breakfast Quesadilla 10
- Blueberry Muffins 10
- Cinnamon Sugar Donut Holes 11
- 12 Breakfast Empanadas 11
- Easy Breakfast Wraps 12
- Breakfast Hash Browns 12
- Egg Cups with Peppers 13
- Egg Loaded Avocado 13
- Air Fryer Breakfast Quesadillas 13
- Air Fryer Veggie Omelet 14
- Double Cherry Mini Egg Rolls 14
- Maple Cinnamon Oatmeal Breakfast Cookies 15
- 21 Flapjacks with Strawberry Jam 15

Chapter 2: Main Recipes 16
- Thai Basil Chicken 16
- Italian Sausage and Peppers 16
- Brazilian Churrasco Skewers 16
- Argentine Beef Empanadas 17
- Malaysian Satay Chicken 18
- Brazilian Feijoada 18
- Indian Chicken Tikka Masala 19
- Mexican Carne Asada 19
- Lebanese Kofta Kebabs 20
- 10 Vegan Katsu Curry 20
- Peruvian Chicken 21
- Chimichurri Steak 21
- Vietnamese Lemongrass Pork 22
- Moroccan Chicken Tagine 22
- Mexican Street Corn 23
- Paneer Tikka 23

Vegan Quinoa and Sweet Potato Burgers ... 24
Vegan Shepherd's Pie ... 25
Chickpea and Spinach Curry ... 25
Air Fryer Veggie "Fried" Rice ... 26

Chapter 3: Fish and Seafood 27
Fish Tacos ... 27
Cajun Shrimp and Grits ... 27
Crispy Calamari Rings ... 28
Garlic Butter Scallops ... 28
Baja Fish Fillet ... 29
Teriyaki Glazed Salmon ... 29
Mediterranean Grilled Octopus ... 30
Jamaican Brown Stew Fish ... 30
Spicy Shrimp and Broccoli ... 31
Thai Sweet Chili Salmon ... 32
Lemon Garlic Shrimp ... 32
Sesame Ginger Tuna ... 32
Cajun Salmon Patties ... 33
Brazilian Moqueca de Peixe (Fish Stew) ... 33
Spanish Paella with Seafood ... 34
Cajun Shrimp Alfredo ... 35
Sriracha Honey Glazed Salmon ... 35
Singaporean Chili Crab ... 36

Chapter 4: Poultry & Meat Recipes   37
Argentinian Chimichurri Chicken ... 37
Turkish Kofta Kebabs ... 37
Brazilian Picanha Steak ... 38
Greek Souvlaki Pork Skewers ... 38

Italian Breaded Chicken Cutlets ... 38
Chinese Honey Sesame Chicken ... 39
Moroccan Lamb Meatballs ... 40
Thai Basil Pork Stir Fry ... 40
Jamaican Beef Patty ... 41
Greek Lamb Chops ... 42
Brazilian Chicken Heart Skewers ... 42
Jamaican Curry Goat ... 43
Korean BBQ Beef Short Ribs ... 43
Chinese Five Spice Pork Tenderloin ... 44
Chicken Fried Steak ... 45
Chicken Parmesan ... 45
Breaded Veal Cutlets ... 46
Southern Fried Chicken ... 46
Crispy Pork Schnitzel ... 47
Chicken Nuggets ... 48

Chapter 5: Healthy Vegetables and Sides 49
Cauliflower "Steak" ... 49
Broccoli and Carrots ... 49
Green Beans with Garlic ... 49
Roasted Garlic Mushrooms ... 50
Eggplant Fries ... 50
Spicy Okra ... 51
Butternut Squash Wedges ... 51
Roasted Carrot Fries ... 51
Garlic Parmesan Broccoli ... 52
Cinnamon Roasted Sweet Potatoes ... 52
Sautéed Spinach with Garlic ... 52

Grilled Portobello Mushrooms 53
Roasted Balsamic Brussel Sprouts 53
Sesame Soy Broccoli 53
Roasted Garlic and Rosemary Potatoes 54
Lemon Herb Roasted Cauliflower 54
Parmesan Roasted Acorn Squash 55
Curried Cauliflower Rice 55

Chapter 6: Fast and Easy Everyday Favourites 56

Grilled Cheese................................. 56
Bacon Wrapped Shrimp 56
Mozzarella Sticks 56
BBQ Chicken Legs 57
Garlic Bread 57
Crispy Fried Chicken 57
Baked Potatoes 58
Grilled Burgers 58
Nachos... 59
Onion Rings 59
Crispy Fried Fish.............................. 60
Cheesy Garlic Bread 60
Beef Taquitos 61
Fish Sticks 61
Popcorn Chicken.............................. 62
Buffalo Cauliflower........................... 62
Chicken Quesadillas 63
Mini Pizzas 63
Jalapeno Poppers............................. 63
Crab Cakes 64

Chapter 7: Appetisers 65

Crab Rangoon 65
Falafel Balls 65
Loaded Potato Skins 66
Fried Pickles 66
Panko Crusted Shrimp 66
Spinach and Feta Stuffed Mushrooms 67
Coconut Chicken Strips 67
Greek Feta Fries 68
Zucchini Fritters 68
Vietnamese Spring Rolls...................... 69
Caprese Stuffed Mushrooms 69
Pork Dumplings 70
Double Bean Chilli 70
Aubergine Burgers 71
Cheesy Polenta Stacks 71

Chapter 8: Snacks and Desserts ... 72

Strawberry Cheesecake Egg Rolls 72
Mini Apple Pies 72
S'mores 73
Blueberry Hand Pies 73
Nutella-Stuffed French Toast 73
Chocolate Lava Cakes......................... 74
Peanut Butter Cupcakes 74
Lemon Bars................................... 75
Peach Cobbler 75
Banana Bread 76
Cherry Turnovers 76
Bread Pudding with Caramel Sauce 77

Mini Cheesecakes	77
Pumpkin Spice Donut Holes	78
Almond Biscotti	78
Oreo Cheesecake Bites	79

Chapter 9: Staples, Sauces, Dips, and Dressings 80

Homemade Tater Tots	80
Roasted Red Pepper Hummus	80
Cilantro Lime Rice	81
Hummus Dip With Veggie Crisps	81
Peanut Butter Oatmeal Bake	81
Egg Fried Rice	82
Honey Mustard Dressing	82
Tahini Sauce	82
Baked Camembert With Croutons	83
Pesto Sauce	83
Spicy Sriracha Mayo	84
Basil Aioli	84
Harissa Sauce	84
Chinese Dumpling Sauce	85
Creamy Avocado Dressing	85
Basil Walnut Pesto	85
Coconut Curry Sauce	86
Refried Bean Dip	86

Introduction

From my earliest memories of baking fairy cakes with my grandmother to the more intricate dishes I prepare today, cooking has always held a special place in my heart. As I've grown older, my passion for cooking has only deepened, leading me on a journey of culinary exploration, where I eagerly delve into different cuisines, experiment with flavors, and master new techniques.

When my family and I moved to the UK, a whole new world of culinary possibilities opened up before me. I was excited to immerse myself in the local ingredients and cooking methods unique to this region. From the classic fish and chips to the comforting shepherd's pie, I was determined to learn and master it all.

During the challenging times of the pandemic lockdowns, like many others, I sought ways to maintain a healthy diet without compromising on taste. That's when I stumbled upon the game-changing Ninja Dual Zone air fryer. This remarkable appliance allowed me to create delectable, crispy dishes with just a fraction of the oil typically required for frying.

As I experimented with various recipes, I soon discovered the incredible versatility of the Ninja Dual Zone air fryer. Inspired by my culinary adventures, I began compiling my very own recipe book, exclusively designed for this innovative kitchen companion. Within its pages, you'll find a diverse collection of easy-to-follow recipes, meticulously crafted to help you whip up quick, healthy meals without any unnecessary hassle.

Whether you're looking for a delightful breakfast, a hearty dinner, tempting appetisers, or indulgent desserts, my recipe book has you covered. Each recipe has been carefully tested to ensure that they not only nourish your body but also delight your taste buds with exceptional flavours.

So, whether you're a seasoned chef or just embarking on your culinary journey, I warmly invite you to join me in embracing the exciting world of the Ninja Dual Zone air fryer. With my recipe book in hand and this cutting-edge appliance at your disposal, you'll be empowered to create an array of mouthwatering dishes with confidence and ease. Together, let's unlock the boundless possibilities of air frying and embark on a culinary adventure like no other!

Getting to know the Ninja Dual Zone

Congratulations on your latest addition to the kitchen, the Ninja Dual Zone air fryer! I understand that embracing a new kitchen appliance can sometimes feel overwhelming, but fear not! I'm here to assist you in making the most out of your investment. The best part is, using an air fryer is a breeze, requiring no more complexity than operating a standard microwave.

In my specially crafted recipe book tailored for the Ninja Dual Zone air fryer, you'll find step-by-step instructions that make cooking a delight. With adjusted cooking times and temperatures, you'll effortlessly whip up delectable dishes that strike the perfect balance between health and satisfaction.

The versatility of the Ninja Dual Zone air fryer is truly remarkable. From crispy chicken wings and perfectly golden French fries to delightful baked goods and mouth watering vegetables, this appliance does it all. The beauty lies in its ability to achieve that coveted crispy texture without the excessive oil and mess associated with traditional frying.

So, banish any hesitation you may have about your new air fryer. Armed with my recipe book and the user-friendly Ninja Dual Zone air fryer, you'll swiftly become a culinary maestro. Let's embark on this thrilling cooking journey together, uncovering a world of incredible dishes waiting to be savoured!

So, What is the Ninja Dual Zone Air Fryer?

If you're seeking a kitchen appliance that offers versatility and convenience, look no further than the Ninja Dual Zone air fryer. This remarkable device features two separate cooking areas, each with adjustable temperatures and settings, allowing you to prepare multiple dishes simultaneously without compromising on taste or quality.

With its preset modes, the Ninja Dual Zone air fryer takes the guesswork out of cooking, making it a perfect choice for cooks of all skill levels. Whether you're craving crispy chicken wings, golden French fries, succulent roasts, quick reheats, healthy dehydrated snacks, or delectable baked goods, this appliance has got you covered.

What sets this air fryer apart is its ability to cater to your entire meal. Imagine effortlessly cooking a mouthwatering roast in one zone while keeping your sides warm and perfectly crispy in the other. It's like having a personal chef, ensuring every element of your meal is cooked to perfection without the need for constant monitoring.

Inside this recipe book, you'll find an entire chapter dedicated to desserts, showcasing the Ninja Dual Zone's prowess as the ultimate party companion. But it doesn't stop there. From weekday dinners to weekend gatherings, this appliance will transform your culinary creations into restaurant-quality meals that will impress your family and friends.

So, whether you're a seasoned chef or just beginning your culinary journey, let's delve into the endless possibilities of the Ninja Dual Zone air fryer together. Get ready to elevate your cooking game and embark on a flavorful adventure that will delight your taste buds and leave you with unforgettable dining experiences.

Why Choose the Ninja Dual Zone?

With the growing popularity of air fryers, it can be overwhelming to navigate the sea of options available. However, the Ninja Dual Zone air fryer stands apart as a standout choice for your kitchen. What sets it apart is its unique feature of two separate cooking areas, allowing you to simultaneously prepare different dishes at varying temperatures. This is a game-changer, especially for families with diverse dietary needs or for those who love hosting gatherings with a wide array of culinary preferences.

But the Ninja Dual Zone offers more than just convenience—it also provides a range of accessories to elevate your cooking experience. From baking cakes to crafting delectable pizzas, the available accessories from the Ninja store open up a world of culinary possibilities. And the best part? Cleaning up after a multi-course meal is a breeze, ensuring that your cooking adventures remain enjoyable from start to finish.

Choosing the Ninja Dual Zone air fryer is an investment in flexibility and versatility in the kitchen. And now, with the addition of this recipe book, you can take your air frying skills to new heights and amaze your loved ones with a repertoire of delicious and wholesome meals. So, seize the opportunity, get your hands on the Ninja Dual Zone air fryer, and embark on a culinary journey filled with flavour, creativity, and satisfaction.

The Benefits of the Ninja Dual Zone Air Fryer

In today's era, finding ways to conserve energy and cut down on expenses is of paramount importance. Enter the Ninja Dual Zone air fryer, a remarkable solution that not only allows you to cook meals swiftly and efficiently but also helps reduce your electricity bills. I was astounded by how much time I saved using the Ninja Dual Zone, as it can cook food 75% faster than a traditional oven, resulting in significantly reduced energy consumption.

The Ninja Dual Zone's impressive 7.5L capacity

is another standout feature, making it perfect for preparing large family meals or entertaining guests. Gone are the days of worrying about cooking in multiple batches—I was able to cook an entire roast dinner in one go. The dual cooking zones are a game-changer, allowing me to effortlessly prepare multiple dishes at different temperatures and settings within a single appliance, without the hassle of managing multiple pots and pans.

Not only is the Ninja Dual Zone a time and energy-saving marvel, but it also promotes healthier cooking practices. By utilising 75% less fat than traditional cooking methods, it empowers you to prepare wholesome meals for your loved ones without compromising on flavour.

Within this recipe book, you'll discover a diverse range of dishes that can be quickly and easily prepared using the Ninja Dual Zone. From delectable chicken wings to crispy vegetables and delightful desserts, each recipe has been carefully crafted to maximise the features of the Ninja Dual Zone, including its convenient preset modes. Even if you're new to cooking, these recipes ensure that you can effortlessly create mouth-watering meals with confidence.

In conclusion, I wholeheartedly recommend the Ninja Dual Zone air fryer to anyone seeking a cost-effective, energy-efficient, and health-conscious method of cooking. With the invaluable addition of this recipe book, you'll have access to a treasure trove of delectable dishes that your family and friends will adore, all while saving money and savouring the incredible flavours. Don't delay—let the Ninja Dual Zone revolutionise your culinary journey today!

How to Clean the Ninja Dual Zone Air Fryer?

As an avid cooking enthusiast, I often find myself hesitant to prepare certain dishes due to the daunting task of cleaning up afterwards. However, the Ninja Dual Zone air fryer has completely transformed my cleaning experience!

Cleaning the Ninja Dual Zone is an absolute breeze thanks to its non-stick compartments. These surfaces make it incredibly easy to wipe away any residue or food particles. What's more, the compartments are dishwasher safe, allowing for effortless cleaning with the simple convenience of your dishwasher. To further simplify clean-up, many of the recipes in this cookbook recommend using non-stick cooking spray or lining the trays with baking paper.

When it comes to tidying up the Ninja Dual Zone, I recommend either hand washing the parts with hot soapy water and a sponge, or conveniently placing them in the dishwasher. Unlike other air fryer brands, the Ninja Dual Zone even allows for the use of baking paper or aluminium foil during cooking, which not only saves time but also simplifies the cleaning process.

For those stubborn, burnt-on messes that occasionally occur, Ninja provides a specialised cleaning brush to tackle even the toughest grime. By using the Ninja cleaning brush with hot soapy water, you can effortlessly restore the pristine condition of your air fryer.

For added convenience, consider purchasing tray liners specifically designed for the Ninja Dual Zone. These liners not only streamline the clean-up process but also minimise the need for baking paper or aluminium foil, promoting environmental sustainability.

With the Ninja Dual Zone air fryer, the dread of post-cooking clean-up becomes a thing of the past. Embrace the opportunity to try out those recipes you've been avoiding, as the Ninja Dual Zone ensures that cleaning up is a breeze. So, unleash your culinary creativity and enjoy the remarkable ease of clean-up with the Ninja Dual Zone air fryer!

Possible Risks

When incorporating an air fryer into your cooking routine, it is crucial to prioritise safety and take necessary precautions to protect yourself and those around you. One common concern among air fryer users revolves around the possibility of burning food due to the high cooking temperatures involved.

To mitigate this risk, it is essential to closely monitor new recipes and stick to tried-and-tested ones to minimise the chances of burning. Regularly checking the food as it cooks will help ensure that it doesn't become overcooked.

Another consideration that has been raised regarding air frying is the potential formation of cholesterol oxidation products (COPs) when certain foods are cooked at high temperatures. While no conclusive evidence directly links the Ninja Dual Zone air fryer or air-fried foods to the production of COPs, it is important to stay informed about the associated risks and exercise caution.

Despite these potential risks, air fryers offer numerous benefits, such as the ability to prepare delicious and crispy meals with minimal added oil. When used responsibly and in accordance with healthy cooking practices, the Ninja Dual Zone air fryer can be a valuable asset in any kitchen.

In conclusion, it is crucial to educate yourself about the potential risks and benefits of air fryer usage and take appropriate precautions to ensure safe and healthy cooking. By remaining vigilant and utilising responsible cooking practices, you can enjoy all the advantages of the Ninja Dual Zone air fryer without undue concern over potential risks.

Tips and Tricks to Using the Ninja Dual Zone Air Fryer

For those who prioritise healthy cooking, the Ninja Dual Zone air fryer is an indispensable addition to the kitchen. Its ability to cook food using little to no oil makes it a fantastic tool for preparing delicious and nutritious meals. To optimise your cooking experience, we've compiled a collection of valuable tips and tricks that will help you achieve exceptional results with your air fryer.

To begin, consider exploring a range of accessories designed to enhance your culinary endeavours. Items such as racks, silicone oven mitts, and other tools can significantly improve your cooking outcomes, especially when preparing multiple dishes simultaneously.

Preheating your air fryer is another tip worth noting, as it promotes more even cooking, particularly for baked goods. Additionally, it's important to remember that different foods require specific cooking temperatures and durations. To ensure your meals are cooked to perfection, be sure to follow the instructions provided in your recipe book or reliable online guides.

Avoid overcrowding the drawers of your Ninja Dual Zone air fryer, as this can result in uneven cooking or difficulties with drawer closure. Instead, opt for smaller batch sizes or utilise the racks provided with your air fryer. This will allow you to cook larger quantities without compromising cooking quality or air circulation.

Regular cleaning is essential to keep your air fryer in top-notch condition. Fortunately, the non-stick surfaces of the Ninja Dual Zone air fryer make cleaning a breeze. Simply wipe it down with a damp cloth or sponge after each use. It's also recommended to clean the accompanying accessories, such as racks and silicone mitts, to maintain their longevity.

Lastly, embrace your culinary curiosity and experiment with various recipes and ingredients. The versatility of the Ninja Dual Zone air fryer allows for an extensive range of dishes. From crispy chicken wings to delectable vegetables and even delectable desserts like donuts or cakes, the possibilities are limitless. Let your creativity shine and delight your loved ones with mouthwatering creations.

In conclusion, investing in the Ninja Dual Zone air fryer empowers you to effortlessly prepare healthy and scrumptious meals without the hassle or mess. By incorporating these tips and tricks into your cooking routine, you'll unlock the full potential of your air fryer and delight in culinary masterpieces that will impress even the most discerning palates.

FAQs

Is it safe to remove the drawer while food is cooking in the Ninja Dual Zone Air Fryer?

Absolutely! In fact, it is recommended to remove the drawer halfway through cooking to shake or flip the food for even cooking. You can also open the drawer a few times towards the end of the cooking time to check the doneness of the food.

Does the exterior of the Ninja Dual Zone Air Fryer get hot during cooking?

Yes, the outer part of the air fryer does get warm during cooking. However, the handles and control panel remain safe to touch. To ensure safety, you can use oven mitts or silicone gloves if you prefer.

Should I thaw frozen foods before placing them in the Ninja Dual Zone Air Fryer?

It depends on the food. It is best to follow the instructions on the packaging of the frozen food. In general, some frozen foods may require thawing before cooking, while others can be cooked directly from frozen. It is important to ensure that frozen food is cooked thoroughly before serving.

Can I adjust the settings on the Ninja Dual Zone Air Fryer while it is in operation?

Absolutely! You can adjust settings such as temperature and cooking time while the food is cooking in the air fryer. This flexibility allows you to make any necessary adjustments for desired cooking results.

Do I need to clean the air fryer after every use?

While it is not mandatory to clean the air fryer after every use, it is recommended to remove any leftover crumbs or food particles. This helps prevent them from burning and potentially causing damage to the trays over time. If you use liners or foil, you may be able to reduce the frequency of cleaning, but it is always good practice to check for any residue before cooking again.

Can an air fryer overheat?

It is possible for an air fryer to overheat, especially if it is not given enough space for proper air circulation. It is generally recommended to leave approximately 6 inches of space around the air fryer during operation to prevent overheating.

How can I ensure that meat is cooked safely in the Ninja Dual Zone Air Fryer?

The Ninja website offers a specific thermometer for checking the doneness of meat. Alternatively, you can use a regular meat thermometer to ensure that beef, pork, lamb, chicken, seafood, and other meats reach the appropriate internal temperature for safe consumption.

Can I boil water in the Ninja Dual Zone Air Fryer?

Boiling water in the air fryer is not recommended due to safety concerns. The fan inside the air fryer may cause water to splash into the internal parts, potentially leading to malfunctions. It is safer to use a kettle or stovetop for boiling water.

Can I use toothpicks or wooden skewers in the Ninja Dual Zone Air Fryer?

Yes, you can use toothpicks or wooden skewers in the air fryer. However, it is advisable to soak them in water for approximately 15 minutes before using them to prevent them from burning during the cooking process.

Does the Ninja Dual Zone Air Fryer produce cooking odours?

One of the advantages of the Ninja Dual Zone Air Fryer is its ability to minimise cooking odours. Even when cooking strong-smelling foods like fish, the air fryer significantly reduces the likelihood of lingering odours, allowing you to enjoy a pleasant cooking and dining experience.

Can I layer food in the Ninja Dual Zone Air Fryer?

While it is recommended to cook meat in a single layer for optimal results, you can layer foods like chips or vegetables in the air fryer. However, it is important to shake or flip the food halfway through the cooking process to ensure even cooking. With the dual-zone feature, you can also cook different types of food simultaneously in separate zones, further enhancing the versatility of the air fryer.

Chapter 1: Breakfast Recipes

Churro Waffles

Serves: 4
Prep time: 15 minutes / Cook time: 10 minutes

Ingredients:

For the churro waffle batter:
- 200g all-purpose flour
- 30g granulated sugar
- 2 tsp baking powder
- 1/2 tsp salt
- 1 tsp ground cinnamon
- 240 ml whole milk
- 2 large eggs
- 60ml vegetable oil
- 1 tsp vanilla extract

For the cinnamon sugar coating:
- 80g granulated sugar
- 2 tsp ground cinnamon
- 60g unsalted butter, melted

For serving:
- Maple syrup or chocolate sauce (optional)

Preparation instructions:

1. Preheat the Ninja Dual Zone Air Fryer to 180°C on zone 1 for 5 minutes.
2. In a large bowl, whisk together the flour, sugar, baking powder, salt, and cinnamon.
3. In a separate bowl, whisk together the milk, eggs, vegetable oil, and vanilla extract.
4. Pour the wet ingredients into the dry ingredients and stir until just combined. Be careful not to overmix; a few lumps are fine.
5. Lightly grease the waffle plates of the air fryer with cooking spray or oil.
6. Divide the churro waffle batter evenly among the waffle plates and close the lid.
7. Cook the waffles in zone 1 at 180°C for about 8-10 minutes or until golden brown and crispy.
8. While the waffles are cooking, prepare the cinnamon sugar coating. In a shallow bowl, combine the granulated sugar and ground cinnamon.
9. Remove the cooked waffles from the air fryer and brush them with melted butter. Immediately coat each waffle in the cinnamon sugar mixture until fully coated.
10. Serve the churro waffles warm with a drizzle of maple syrup or chocolate sauce, if desired.

Breakfast Pita

Serves: 2
Prep time: 15 minutes / Cook time: 10 minutes

Ingredients:
- 2 whole wheat pitas
- 4 large eggs
- 60ml whole milk
- 1/4 tsp garlic powder
- 1/4 tsp onion powder
- Salt and black pepper, to taste
- 100g diced cooked bacon
- 50g shredded cheddar cheese
- 1 small tomato, diced
- 2 tbsp chopped fresh parsley or chives (optional)

Preparation instructions:

1. Preheat the Ninja Dual Zone Air Fryer to 180°C on zone 1 for 5 minutes.
2. In a bowl, whisk together the eggs, whole milk, garlic powder, onion powder, salt, and black pepper.
3. Place the pitas in zone 1 of the air fryer and cook at 180°C for 2-3 minutes to warm them up.
4. Remove the pitas from the air fryer and cut them in half to form pockets.

5. In a separate bowl, combine the diced bacon, shredded cheddar cheese, diced tomato, and chopped fresh parsley or chives (if using).
6. Divide the bacon and cheese mixture evenly among the pita pockets.
7. Pour the egg mixture into each pita pocket, filling them about 3/4 full.
8. Return the filled pitas to the air fryer in zone 1 and cook at 180°C for 8-10 minutes or until the eggs are set and the cheese is melted.
9. Once cooked, remove the breakfast pitas from the air fryer and let them cool for a minute or two.
10. Serve the breakfast pitas warm and enjoy as a delicious and portable morning meal.

Monte Cristo Sandwich

Serves: 2
Prep time: 10 minutes / Cook time: 8 minutes

Ingredients:
- 4 slices of white bread
- 4 slices of ham
- 4 slices of Swiss cheese
- 2 large eggs
- 60ml whole milk
- Salt and black pepper, to taste
- Butter, for spreading
- Raspberry jam, for serving

Preparation instructions:
1. Preheat the Ninja Dual Zone Air Fryer to 180°C on zone 1 for 5 minutes.
2. Assemble the sandwiches by layering a slice of ham and a slice of Swiss cheese between two slices of bread. Repeat to make 2 sandwiches.
3. In a shallow dish, whisk together the eggs, milk, salt, and black pepper.
4. Dip each sandwich into the egg mixture, making sure to coat both sides.
5. Spread butter on both sides of each sandwich.
6. Place the sandwiches in zone 1 of the air fryer and cook at 180°C for 4 minutes.
7. Flip the sandwiches and cook for an additional 4 minutes or until the bread is golden brown and the cheese is melted.
8. Remove the sandwiches from the air fryer and let them cool for a minute.
9. Cut each sandwich diagonally into halves and serve with raspberry jam on the side.

Corn Fritters

Serves: 4
Prep time: 15 minutes / Cook time: 10 minutes

Ingredients:
- 200g canned corn kernels, drained
- 100g all-purpose flour
- 1 tsp baking powder
- 1/2 tsp paprika
- 1/4 tsp salt
- 1/4 tsp black pepper
- 1 large egg
- 60ml whole milk
- 2 spring onions, finely chopped
- Vegetable oil, for frying

Preparation instructions:
1. Preheat the Ninja Dual Zone Air Fryer to 200°C on zone 1 for 5 minutes.
2. In a bowl, combine the corn kernels, flour, baking powder, paprika, salt, and black pepper.
3. In a separate bowl, whisk together the egg and milk.
4. Pour the egg mixture into the corn mixture and stir until well combined.
5. Add the chopped spring onions to the batter and mix well.
6. Lightly grease the air fryer basket with vegetable oil.
7. Spoon tablespoons of the corn batter into the air fryer basket, spacing them apart.

8. Cook the corn fritters in zone 1 at 200°C for 8-10 minutes or until golden brown and crispy.
9. Flip the fritters halfway through the cooking time for even browning.
10. Remove the fritters from the air fryer and let them cool on a wire rack for a few minutes before serving.

Shakshuka

Serves: 2
Prep time: 10 minutes / Cook time: 15 minutes

Ingredients:
- 1 tbsp olive oil
- 1 small onion, chopped
- 1 small red bell pepper, chopped
- 2 cloves of garlic, minced
- 1 tsp ground cumin
- 1 tsp ground paprika
- 1/4 tsp cayenne pepper (optional)
- 400g canned diced tomatoes
- Salt and black pepper, to taste
- 4 large eggs
- Fresh parsley, chopped (for garnish)

Preparation instructions:
1. Preheat the Ninja Dual Zone Air Fryer to 180°C on zone 1 for 5 minutes.
2. Heat the olive oil in a skillet or frying pan over medium heat.
3. Add the chopped onion and bell pepper to the pan and sauté for about 5 minutes until softened.
4. Stir in the minced garlic, ground cumin, ground paprika, and cayenne pepper (if using), and cook for another minute.
5. Pour the canned diced tomatoes into the pan, season with salt and black pepper, and simmer for 5 minutes to thicken the sauce.
6. Transfer the tomato mixture to two individual-sized oven-safe dishes or ramekins.
7. Create wells in the tomato mixture and crack an egg into each well.
8. Place the dishes in zone 1 of the air fryer and cook at 180°C for 10-12 minutes or until the eggs are cooked to your desired doneness.
9. Remove the shakshuka from the air fryer and garnish with freshly chopped parsley.
10. Serve the shakshuka with crusty bread or pita for dipping.

Breakfast Egg Rolls

Serves: 4
Prep time: 20 minutes / Cook time: 10 minutes

Ingredients:
- 8 egg roll wrappers
- 4 large eggs
- 60ml whole milk
- 1/4 tsp garlic powder
- 1/4 tsp onion powder
- Salt and black pepper, to taste
- 100g cooked bacon, crumbled
- 100g shredded cheddar cheese
- 1 small red bell pepper, finely diced
- Vegetable oil, for frying

Preparation instructions:
1. Preheat the Ninja Dual Zone Air Fryer to 200°C on zone 1 for 5 minutes.
2. In a bowl, whisk together the eggs, milk, garlic powder, onion powder, salt, and black pepper.
3. Heat a non-stick skillet over medium heat and scramble the egg mixture until just cooked.
4. Transfer the scrambled eggs to a bowl and let them cool slightly.
5. Add the crumbled bacon, shredded cheddar cheese, and diced red bell pepper to the scrambled eggs, and mix well.
6. Lay an egg roll wrapper on a clean surface and spoon about 2 tablespoons of the egg filling onto the centre of the wrapper.

7. Fold the sides of the wrapper over the filling and roll tightly into a cylinder, sealing the edges with a bit of water.
8. Repeat the process with the remaining egg roll wrappers and filling.
9. Lightly brush or spray the egg rolls with vegetable oil to coat them evenly.
10. Place the egg rolls in zone 1 of the air fryer and cook at 200°C for 8-10 minutes or until golden brown and crispy.
11. Flip the egg rolls halfway through the cooking time for even browning.
12. Remove the egg rolls from the air fryer and let them cool for a few minutes before serving. Serve with your favourite dipping sauce.

Bacon and Egg Breakfast Pockets

Serves: 4
Prep time: 15 minutes / Cook time: 10 minutes

Ingredients:
- 8 slices of bread
- 8 slices of bacon, cooked until crispy
- 4 large eggs
- 60ml whole milk
- Salt and black pepper, to taste
- Butter, for spreading

Preparation instructions:
1. Preheat the Ninja Dual Zone Air Fryer to 180°C on zone 1 for 5 minutes.
2. Cut the crusts off the bread slices and use a rolling pin to flatten them slightly.
3. Place a slice of bacon on each slice of bread.
4. In a bowl, whisk together the eggs, milk, salt, and black pepper.
5. Heat a non-stick skillet over medium heat and scramble the egg mixture until just cooked.
6. Divide the scrambled eggs among the bacon slices on the bread.
7. Fold each slice of bread in half to form a pocket and press the edges to seal.
8. Spread butter on both sides of each breakfast pocket.
9. Place the pockets in zone 1 of the air fryer and cook at 180°C for 5 minutes.
10. Flip the pockets and cook for an additional 5 minutes or until the bread is golden brown and crispy.
11. Remove the breakfast pockets from the air fryer and let them cool for a minute or two.
12. Serve the bacon and egg breakfast pockets warm and enjoy as a delicious handheld breakfast option.

French Toast Sticks

Serves: 4
Prep time: 10 minutes / Cook time: 8 minutes

Ingredients:
- 4 slices of brioche bread, cut into strips
- 2 large eggs
- 60ml whole milk
- 1 tsp vanilla extract
- 1/2 tsp ground cinnamon
- Butter, for greasing
- Maple syrup, for serving

Preparation instructions:
1. Preheat the Ninja Dual Zone Air Fryer to 180°C on zone 1 for 5 minutes.
2. In a shallow dish, whisk together the eggs, milk, vanilla extract, and ground cinnamon.
3. Dip each strip of brioche bread into the egg mixture, coating it on all sides.
4. Lightly grease the air fryer basket with butter.
5. Arrange the dipped bread strips in a single layer in zone 1 of the air fryer.
6. Cook the French toast sticks at 180°C for 4 minutes.
7. Flip the sticks and cook for another 4 minutes or until they are golden brown and crispy.
8. Remove the French toast sticks from the air

fryer and let them cool for a minute.
9. Serve the French toast sticks warm with maple syrup for dipping or drizzling.

Breakfast Quesadilla

Serves: 2
Prep time: 10 minutes / Cook time: 8 minutes

Ingredients:
- 2 large flour tortillas
- 4 large eggs
- 60ml whole milk
- Salt and black pepper, to taste
- 50g shredded cheddar cheese
- 50g cooked bacon, crumbled
- 2 spring onions, chopped
- 1 small tomato, diced
- Salsa or hot sauce, for serving (optional)

Preparation instructions:
1. Preheat the Ninja Dual Zone Air Fryer to 180°C on zone 1 for 5 minutes.
2. In a bowl, whisk together the eggs, milk, salt, and black pepper.
3. Heat a non-stick skillet over medium heat and scramble the egg mixture until just cooked.
4. Place one tortilla on a clean surface and sprinkle half of the shredded cheddar cheese evenly over the tortilla.
5. Spread the scrambled eggs, crumbled bacon, chopped spring onions, and diced tomato over the cheese.
6. Sprinkle the remaining shredded cheddar cheese on top.
7. Place the second tortilla on top to form a quesadilla.
8. Lightly grease the air fryer basket with cooking spray or oil.
9. Carefully transfer the quesadilla to zone 1 of the air fryer and cook at 180°C for 4 minutes.
10. Flip the quesadilla and cook for an additional 4 minutes or until the cheese is melted and the tortilla is golden brown and crispy.
11. Remove the breakfast quesadilla from the air fryer and let it cool for a minute or two.
12. Slice the quesadilla into wedges and serve with salsa or hot sauce, if desired.

Blueberry Muffins

Serves: 12
Prep time: 15 minutes / Cook time: 18 minutes

Ingredients:
- 200g all-purpose flour
- 100g granulated sugar
- 2 tsp baking powder
- 1/4 tsp salt
- 120ml whole milk
- 60ml vegetable oil
- 1 large egg
- 1 tsp vanilla extract
- 150g fresh blueberries

Preparation instructions:
1. Preheat the Ninja Dual Zone Air Fryer to 180°C on zone 1 for 5 minutes.
2. In a large bowl, whisk together the flour, sugar, baking powder, and salt.
3. In a separate bowl, whisk together the milk, vegetable oil, egg, and vanilla extract.
4. Pour the wet ingredients into the dry ingredients and stir until just combined. Do not overmix.
5. Gently fold in the fresh blueberries.
6. Line a muffin tin with paper liners.
7. Spoon the muffin batter into the paper liners, filling each about 3/4 full.
8. Place the muffin tin in zone 1 of the air fryer and cook at 180°C for 16-18 minutes or until a toothpick inserted into the centre of a muffin comes out clean.

9. Remove the blueberry muffins from the air fryer and let them cool in the muffin tin for a few minutes before transferring to a wire rack to cool completely.

Cinnamon Sugar Donut Holes

Serves: 4
Prep time: 10 minutes / Cook time: 6 minutes

Ingredients:
- 150g all-purpose flour
- 50g granulated sugar
- 1 tsp baking powder
- 1/4 tsp salt
- 1/4 tsp ground cinnamon
- 60ml whole milk
- 1 large egg
- 1 tsp vanilla extract
- 60g unsalted butter, melted
- 50g granulated sugar (for coating)
- 1 tsp ground cinnamon (for coating)
- Vegetable oil, for frying

Preparation instructions:
1. Preheat the Ninja Dual Zone Air Fryer to 180°C on zone 1 for 5 minutes.
2. In a large bowl, whisk together the flour, sugar, baking powder, salt, and ground cinnamon.
3. In a separate bowl, whisk together the milk, egg, vanilla extract, and melted butter.
4. Pour the wet ingredients into the dry ingredients and stir until just combined. Do not overmix.
5. Lightly grease your hands with oil and roll the dough into small balls, about 2-3 cm in diameter.
6. In a shallow dish, combine the granulated sugar and ground cinnamon for coating.
7. Drop a few donut holes into the dish of cinnamon sugar and roll them around to coat them evenly. Set aside.
8. Lightly grease the air fryer basket with oil.
9. Place the donut holes in zone 1 of the air fryer and cook at 180°C for 5-6 minutes or until they are golden brown and cooked through.
10. Remove the donut holes from the air fryer and let them cool for a minute.
11. Repeat the cooking process with the remaining donut holes.
12. Serve the cinnamon sugar donut holes warm and enjoy!

12 Breakfast Empanadas

Serves: 4
Prep time: 25 minutes / Cook time: 12 minutes

Ingredients:
- 250g all-purpose flour
- 1/2 tsp salt
- 120g unsalted butter, cold and diced
- 60ml cold water
- 4 large eggs
- 100g cooked breakfast sausage, crumbled
- 50g shredded cheddar cheese
- 2 spring onions, chopped
- Salt and black pepper, to taste
- Vegetable oil, for frying

Preparation instructions:
1. Preheat the Ninja Dual Zone Air Fryer to 180°C on zone 1 for 5 minutes.
2. In a large bowl, whisk together the flour and salt.
3. Add the cold diced butter to the bowl and use a pastry cutter or your fingers to cut the butter into the flour until the mixture resembles coarse crumbs.
4. Gradually add the cold water to the bowl and mix until the dough comes together.
5. Turn the dough out onto a lightly floured surface and knead it a few times until smooth.

6. Divide the dough into 4 equal portions and roll each portion into a circle about 15 cm in diameter.
7. In a bowl, beat one egg and brush the edges of each dough circle with the beaten egg.
8. In a separate bowl, combine the crumbled breakfast sausage, shredded cheddar cheese, chopped spring onions, salt, and black pepper.
9. Place a portion of the sausage and cheese filling on one half of each dough circle, leaving a small border around the edges.
10. Fold the other half of the dough over the filling to form a half-moon shape.
11. Use a fork to press and seal the edges of each empanada.
12. Lightly grease the air fryer basket with oil.
13. Place the empanadas in zone 1 of the air fryer and cook at 180°C for 10-12 minutes or until they are golden brown and crispy.
14. Remove the breakfast empanadas from the air fryer and let them cool for a few minutes before serving.

Easy Breakfast Wraps

Serves 5
Prep time: 10 minutes / Cook time: 21 minutes

Ingredients

- 400g breakfast sausage, sliced
- 500g button mushrooms, cut in quarters
- 1 tsp olive oil
- Sea salt and ground black pepper, to taste
- 1/2 tsp garlic powder
- 5 tortilla wraps
- 1 bell pepper, seeded and sliced
- 100g canned chickpeas, drained

Preparation Instructions

1. Insert a crisper plate in both drawers. Spray the plates with nonstick cooking oil.
2. Add breakfast sausage to the zone 1 drawer.
3. Toss the mushrooms with olive oil, salt, black pepper, and garlic powder; now, add the mushrooms to the zone 2 drawer.
4. Select zone 1 and pair it with "AIR FRY" at 200°C for 16 minutes. Select zone 2 and pair it with "AIR FRY" at 200°C for 12 minutes
5. Select "SYNC" followed by the "START/STOP" button. At the halfway point, shake your food or toss it with silicone-tipped tongs to promote even cooking.
6. To assemble your wraps: divide the sausages, mushrooms, pepper, and chickpeas between tortilla wraps; wrap them up.
7. Add wraps to the drawers of your Ninja Foodi. Select "REHEAT" at 170°C for 5 minutes. Devour!

Breakfast Hash Browns

Serves 4
Prep time: 20 minutes / Cook time: 15 minutes

Ingredients

- 500g medium-sized potatoes (such as Maris Pipers or King Edward)
- Sea salt and ground black pepper, to taste
- 1 tsp cayenne pepper
- 50g butter, melted

Preparation Instructions

1. Boil the potatoes for 10 minutes; drain until they are cool enough to handle. Peel the potatoes and coarsely grate them into a bowl. Season your potatoes with salt and pepper.
2. Add the melted butter and mix to combine; shape the mixture into 7-8 patties. Insert a crisper plate in both drawers.
3. Spray the plates with nonstick cooking oil. Arrange hash browns on crisper plates
4. Select zone 1 and pair it with "AIR FRY" at 200°C for 15 minutes. Select "MATCH" followed by the "START/STOP" button.
5. At the halfway point, turn the hash browns over with silicone-tipped tongs. Reinsert

drawers to resume cooking.
6. Serve warm and enjoy!

Egg Cups with Peppers

Serves 4
Prep time: 10 minutes / Cook time: 12 minutes

Ingredients
- 6 whole eggs
- 100g double cream
- 2 medium bell peppers, seeded and chopped
- 1/2 tsp chilli flakes
- Sea salt and ground black pepper, to taste

Preparation Instructions
1. Remove a crisper plate from your Nina Foodi. Preheat the Ninja Foodi to 180°C for 5 minutes. Very lightly butter 8 muffin cases.
2. In a mixing bowl, thoroughly combine all the ingredients.
3. Spoon the mixture into the prepared muffin cases. Place 4 muffin cases in each drawer.
4. Select zone 1 and pair it with "BAKE" at 180°C for 12 minutes. Select "MATCH" followed by the "START/STOP" button. Bon appétit!

Egg Loaded Avocado

Serves 2
Prep time: 3 minutes / Cook time: 10 minutes

Ingredients
- 2 large avocados
- 4 medium sized eggs
- 40g sesame seed
- ¼ tsp sea salt
- ¼ tsp ground black pepper
- 2 tbsp avocado oil
- Tomato Ketchup (to drizzle)

Preparation Instructions
1. Halve the avocados and remove the centre seed
2. Using a spoon, carefully extract the edible fruit content, without breaking it
3. Drizzle avocado oil in the cavities and outer layers of the avocado halves
4. Crack the eggs and pour all of the content into the cavity of the avocados
5. Season the egg filled avocado halves with salt and pepper
6. Place two egg filled avocado halves into each container tray of the ninja duel zone
7. Select the 'air fry' at 180°C for 10 minutes
8. Select 'MATCHED' followed by 'START/STOP' to initiate the air frying process
9. Retrieve the egg filled avocados and drizzle tomato ketchup on top before serving

Air Fryer Breakfast Quesadillas

Serves 2
Prep time: 4 minutes / Cook time: 8 minutes

Ingredients:
- Tortillas
- 2 Eggs
- 50g Cheese
- Sour Cream, Guacamole etc

Preparation Procedures:
1. Preheat your Ninja Dual Zone Air Fryer at 175 degrees Celsius. That is the perfect temperature for cooking quesadillas.
2. Take out your fry pan and scramble-fry your eggs for the filling. Set this aside when you're done.
3. Take out the tortillas and place them on a clean and flat surface.
4. Prepare your fillings, i.e. the scrambled eggs, and cheese. Spread the scrambled eggs on one half of the tortilla flat.
5. Sprinkle the other half with cheese and fold the tortilla in half.
6. Prepare your Ninja Dual Zone Air Fryer

drawers by spraying the non-stick plates with cooking spray or using parchment paper. This will prevent the tortillas from sticking and would aid easy cleaning too.

7. Arrange the quesadillas with enough space in between them on the non-stick plates. The space in between is to ensure the quesadillas cook evenly.
8. Place a heavy oven resistant object or even stick toothpicks down the quesadillas to keep the tortillas closed.
9. Select the "AIR FRY" option and airfry the quesadillas for about 8 minutes. The quesadillas are ready when the tortillas become golden brown and the cheese is melted.
10. Take the quesadillas out and serve with sour cream, guacamole, or any of your favorite cream toppings.

Air Fryer Veggie Omelet

Serves 2
Prep time: 4 minutes / Cook time: 10 minutes

Ingredients:
- Eggs
- Onions
- Mushrooms
- Cherry Tomatoes (Chopped)
- Shredded cheese

Preparation Procedures

1. Preheat the Ninja Dual Zone Air Fryer to a temperature of 200oC.
2. Take out a bowl and break the eggs into it. Add salt and pepper exactly how you like it and keep whisking.
3. Put in the toppings, i.e. mushrooms, chopped tomatoes and onions.
4. Keep whisking the egg mixture lightly and pour it into an oil-brushed oven resistant pan. If you have some parchment paper, line your baking pan with it to aid cleaning and easy removal.
5. Set your Ninja Dual Zone Air to "Bake" and bake the eggs for 5 minutes, to get a nicely cooked fluffy omelet.
6. If you want a fairly firmer omelet, let it cook for about 6-7 minutes. Go 8-10 for a very solid and well-done omelet.
7. You can check the doneness by inserting a toothpick or a knife into the center; it should come out clean.
8. Carefully remove the baking dish from the Air Fryer. Sprinkle the shredded cheese on top of the omelet while it's still hot, allowing it to melt.
9. Let the omelet cool for a few minutes before slicing it into wedges or squares. Garnish with fresh herbs, if desired.

Double Cherry Mini Egg Rolls

Serves 4
Prep time: 20 minutes / Cook time:10 minutes

Ingredients
- 8 egg roll wrappers
- 75 g dried cherries
- 75 g fresh cherries, pitted and chopped
- 2 tablespoons sugar
- 1/4 teaspoon cinnamon
- 1/4 teaspoon almond extract
- Powdered sugar for dusting
- Vanilla ice cream (optional)

Instructions :

1. Preheat your Ninja Dual Zone air fryer to 190°C.
2. In a bowl, mix together dried cherries, fresh cherries, sugar, cinnamon, and almond extract.
3. Lay an egg roll wrapper on a clean surface, and place 1-2 tablespoons of cherry mixture in the center of the wrapper.
4. Roll the wrapper tightly around the cherry

mixture, tucking in the sides as you go.
5. Repeat with remaining egg roll wrappers and cherry mixture.
6. Place the egg rolls in the air fryer basket, making sure they don't touch each other.
7. Air fry for 8-10 minutes, flipping once halfway through cooking time, until the egg rolls are golden brown and crispy.
8. Remove from air fryer and let cool for a few minutes. Dust with powdered sugar.
9. Serve with vanilla ice cream, if desired.

Maple Cinnamon Oatmeal Breakfast Cookies

Serves 8
Prep time: 5 minutes / Cook time: 5 minutes

Ingredients
- 225g caster sugar
- 115g unsalted butter
- 120g oats
- 1 tsp vanilla extract
- 2 large eggs
- 120g all-purpose flour
- ½ tsp sea salt
- ½ tsp baking powder
- 1 ¼ tsp cinnamon
- 120ml maple syrup
- 1cal olive fry spray

Preparation Instructions
1. Preheat the ninja foodi to 180°C for 5 minutes, then carefully line the ninja foodi zone draws with parchment paper
2. Spray the parchment paper thoroughly
3. Employing a stand mixer and a large bowl, amalgamate the butter, eggs, sugar, and vanilla to form a fluffed mixture
4. Add the salt and the baking powder, then combine it using a fork
5. Toss, mix and press in the oats and maple syrup into the mixture
6. Hand mould 8 cookies and place 4 in each ninja zone draw on top of on top of the parchment paper
7. Select the zones and pair them 'BAKE' function at 180°C for 5 minutes
8. Retrieve the cookies and enjoy.

21 Flapjacks with Strawberry Jam

Serves 4
Prep time: 10 minutes / Cook time: 20minutes

Ingredients
- 300g old-fashioned rolled oats
- 150g brown sugar
- 100g butter, melted
- A pinch of sea salt
- 1/4 tsp cinnamon powder
- 200g peanut butter
- 100g strawberry jam

Instructions :
1. Begin by preheating your ninja foodi air fryer to 175°C. Now, brush two baking tins with nonstick cooking spray.
2. In your processor, mix the rolled oats, sugar, butter, spices, and 100 g of peanut butter; stir until everything is well combined.
3. Spoon the batter into the prepared baking tins. Place dots of the remaining peanut butter and jam on top of the flapjacks.
4. Place one baking tin in each drawer.
5. Select zone 1 and pair it with"BAKE" at 180°C for 20 minutes. Select "MATCH" followed by the "START/STOP" button.
6. Place your flapjacks on a cooling rack for 10 minutes before slicing and serving.
7. Serve hot & enjoy

Chapter 2: Main Recipes

Thai Basil Chicken

Serves: 4
Prep time: 15 minutes / Cook time: 10 minutes

Ingredients:

- 500g boneless, skinless chicken thighs, cut into bite-sized pieces
- 2 tbsp soy sauce
- 1 tbsp oyster sauce
- 1 tbsp fish sauce
- 2 tsp sugar
- 2 cloves garlic, minced
- 1 red chilli, sliced (adjust to taste)
- 1 cup fresh basil leaves
- 2 tbsp vegetable oil

Preparation instructions:

1. In a bowl, combine the soy sauce, oyster sauce, fish sauce, sugar, minced garlic, and sliced chilli. Mix well.
2. Add the chicken thigh pieces to the marinade and toss to coat. Let it marinate for 10 minutes.
3. Preheat the Ninja Dual Zone Air Fryer to 200°C on zone 1 for 5 minutes.
4. Remove the chicken from the marinade, shaking off any excess.
5. Place the chicken in zone 1 of the air fryer and cook at 200°C for 8-10 minutes or until the chicken is cooked through and slightly browned.
6. Heat the vegetable oil in a pan over medium heat. Add the cooked chicken to the pan along with the basil leaves. Stir-fry for an additional minute to wilt the basil leaves.
7. Serve the Thai basil chicken with steamed rice or noodles. Enjoy!

Italian Sausage and Peppers

Serves: 4
Prep time: 10 minutes / Cook time: 15 minutes

Ingredients:

- 400g Italian sausage links
- 2 bell peppers (red, green, or a mix), sliced
- 1 onion, sliced
- 2 cloves garlic, minced
- 2 tbsp olive oil
- 1 tsp dried oregano
- 1/2 tsp dried basil
- Salt and black pepper, to taste

Preparation instructions:

1. Preheat the Ninja Dual Zone Air Fryer to 200°C on zone 1 for 5 minutes.
2. In a bowl, toss the sliced bell peppers and onions with minced garlic, olive oil, dried oregano, dried basil, salt, and black pepper.
3. Place the seasoned bell peppers and onions in zone 1 of the air fryer and cook at 200°C for 10 minutes, stirring halfway through.
4. While the peppers and onions are cooking, heat a separate pan over medium heat. Add the Italian sausage links and cook until browned and cooked through.
5. Once the sausage links are cooked, slice them into bite-sized pieces.
6. Add the sliced sausage to the air fryer basket with the cooked peppers and onions. Cook for an additional 5 minutes at 200°C to heat through.
7. Serve the Italian sausage and peppers on crusty rolls or with pasta. Enjoy!

Brazilian Churrasco Skewers

Serves: 4
Prep time: 20 minutes (+1 hour marinating time) / Cook time: 10 minutes

Ingredients:

- 500g beef sirloin, cut into 2cm cubes
- 1 red bell pepper, cut into 2cm pieces
- 1 green bell pepper, cut into 2cm pieces

- 1 red onion, cut into wedges
- 4 cloves garlic, minced
- 60ml olive oil
- 2 tbsp lime juice
- 2 tbsp soy sauce
- 1 tbsp Worcestershire sauce
- 1 tsp smoked paprika
- 1 tsp ground cumin
- Salt and black pepper, to taste
- Wooden skewers, soaked in water

Preparation instructions:

1. In a bowl, combine the minced garlic, olive oil, lime juice, soy sauce, Worcestershire sauce, smoked paprika, ground cumin, salt, and black pepper to make the marinade.
2. Place the beef cubes in a shallow dish and pour the marinade over them, ensuring the beef is well coated. Cover the dish and let the beef marinate in the refrigerator for at least 1 hour.
3. Preheat the Ninja Dual Zone Air Fryer to 200°C on zone 1 for 5 minutes.
4. Thread the marinated beef cubes onto the soaked wooden skewers, alternating with pieces of red bell pepper, green bell pepper, and red onion.
5. Place the skewers in zone 1 of the air fryer and cook at 200°C for 10 minutes, turning halfway through cooking, or until the beef is cooked to your desired level of doneness and the vegetables are slightly charred.
6. Once cooked, remove the skewers from the air fryer and let them rest for a few minutes before serving.
7. Serve the Brazilian churrasco skewers with steamed rice, a fresh salad, and your favourite chimichurri sauce for dipping. Enjoy the flavorful and tender grilled skewers!

Argentine Beef Empanadas

Serves: 4
Prep time: 30 minutes / Cook time: 15 minutes

Ingredients:
For the dough:
- 250g all-purpose flour
- 1/2 tsp salt
- 100g unsalted butter, cold and cubed
- 60ml water

For the filling:
- 300g ground beef
- 1 small onion, finely chopped
- 1 small red bell pepper, finely chopped
- 2 cloves garlic, minced
- 1 tsp ground cumin
- 1/2 tsp paprika
- Salt and black pepper, to taste
- 2 tbsp olive oil

Preparation instructions:

1. In a large bowl, combine the flour and salt. Add the cubed butter and use your fingers or a pastry cutter to cut the butter into the flour until the mixture resembles coarse crumbs.
2. Gradually add the water, a little at a time, and mix until the dough comes together. Knead the dough lightly on a floured surface until smooth. Wrap in plastic wrap and refrigerate for 30 minutes.
3. In a frying pan, heat the olive oil over medium heat. Add the chopped onion, red bell pepper, and minced garlic, and cook until softened. Add the ground beef and cook until browned. Stir in the ground cumin, paprika, salt, and black pepper. Remove from heat and let the filling cool.
4. Preheat the Ninja Dual Zone Air Fryer to 180°C on zone 1 for 5 minutes.
5. On a lightly floured surface, roll out the dough to a thickness of about 2-3mm. Use a round cutter to cut out circles, approximately 12 cm in diameter.
6. Spoon a portion of the cooled beef filling onto each dough circle. Fold the dough over the filling, pressing the edges together to

seal. You can crimp the edges using a fork for a decorative effect.
7. Place the empanadas in zone 1 of the air fryer and cook at 180°C for 12-15 minutes, or until golden brown and crispy.
8. Once cooked, remove the empanadas from the air fryer and let them cool slightly before serving.

Malaysian Satay Chicken

Serves: 4
Prep time: 30 minutes (+1 hour marinating time) / Cook time: 15 minutes

Ingredients:
- 500g chicken breast, cut into bite-sized pieces
- 4 tbsp peanut butter
- 2 tbsp soy sauce
- 2 tbsp lime juice
- 2 cloves garlic, minced
- 1 tbsp curry powder
- 1 tbsp honey or brown sugar
- 1/2 tsp turmeric powder
- Salt and black pepper, to taste
- Bamboo skewers, soaked in water for 30 minutes

Preparation instructions:
1. In a bowl, combine the peanut butter, soy sauce, lime juice, minced garlic, curry powder, honey or brown sugar, turmeric powder, salt, and black pepper to make the marinade.
2. Add the chicken pieces to the marinade and toss to coat. Cover the bowl and let the chicken marinate in the refrigerator for at least 1 hour.
3. Preheat the Ninja Dual Zone Air Fryer to 200°C on zone 1 for 5 minutes.
4. Thread the marinated chicken onto the soaked bamboo skewers.
5. Place the chicken skewers in zone 1 of the air fryer and cook at 200°C for 12-15 minutes, or until the chicken is cooked through and slightly charred, turning halfway through cooking.
6. Once cooked, remove the chicken skewers from the air fryer and let them rest for a few minutes before serving. Serve with peanut sauce or chilli sauce for dipping.

Brazilian Feijoada

Serves: 4
Prep time: 15 minutes / Cook time: 40 minutes

Ingredients:
- 200g black beans, soaked overnight and drained
- 200g pork shoulder, diced
- 100g smoked sausage, sliced
- 100g bacon, chopped
- 1 onion, chopped
- 2 cloves garlic, minced
- 2 bay leaves
- 1 tbsp olive oil
- 1 tsp ground cumin
- Salt and black pepper, to taste

Preparation instructions:
1. Preheat the Ninja Dual Zone Air Fryer to 180°C on zone 1 for 5 minutes.
2. In a frying pan, heat the olive oil over medium heat. Add the chopped onion and minced garlic, and sauté until translucent.
3. Add the diced pork shoulder, sliced smoked sausage, and chopped bacon to the frying pan. Cook until the meat is browned and the bacon is crispy.
4. Transfer the meat mixture to the air fryer basket. Add the soaked black beans, bay leaves, ground cumin, salt, and black pepper. Toss to combine.
5. Place the air fryer basket in zone 1 and cook at 180°C for 40 minutes, or until the beans are tender and the flavours have melded together.
6. Once cooked, remove the feijoada from the air fryer and let it rest for a few minutes before serving. Serve with white rice and garnish with fresh parsley, if desired.

Indian Chicken Tikka Masala

Serves: 4

Prep time: 30 minutes (+1 hour marinating time) / Cook time: 15 minutes

Ingredients:
- 500g boneless, skinless chicken breasts, cut into bite-sized pieces
- 200g plain yoghurt
- 3 tbsp tomato paste
- 2 cloves garlic, minced
- 2 tsp ground cumin
- 2 tsp ground coriander
- 2 tsp paprika
- 1 tsp ground turmeric
- 1 tsp garam masala
- 1/2 tsp chilli powder (adjust to taste)
- 1 tbsp vegetable oil
- Salt, to taste
- Fresh cilantro, for garnish

Preparation instructions:
1. In a bowl, combine the plain yoghurt, tomato paste, minced garlic, ground cumin, ground coriander, paprika, ground turmeric, garam masala, chilli powder, vegetable oil, and salt to make the marinade.
2. Add the chicken pieces to the marinade and toss to coat. Cover the bowl and let the chicken marinate in the refrigerator for at least 1 hour.
3. Preheat the Ninja Dual Zone Air Fryer to 200°C on zone 1 for 5 minutes.
4. Place the marinated chicken pieces in zone 1 of the air fryer and cook at 200°C for 12-15 minutes, or until the chicken is cooked through and slightly charred, turning halfway through cooking.
5. Once cooked, remove the chicken from the air fryer and let it rest for a few minutes. Garnish with fresh cilantro before serving. Serve with steamed rice and naan bread.

Mexican Carne Asada

Serves: 4

Prep time: 30 minutes (+1 hour marinating time) / Cook time: 10 minutes

Ingredients:
- 500g beef steak (such as flank steak or skirt steak)
- 2 tbsp lime juice
- 2 tbsp orange juice
- 2 cloves garlic, minced
- 1 tsp ground cumin
- 1 tsp chilli powder
- 1 tsp smoked paprika
- 1 tbsp vegetable oil
- Salt and black pepper, to taste
- Fresh cilantro, for garnish
- Lime wedges, for serving

Preparation instructions:
1. In a bowl, combine the lime juice, orange juice, minced garlic, ground cumin, chilli powder, smoked paprika, vegetable oil, salt, and black pepper to make the marinade.
2. Place the beef steak in a shallow dish and pour the marinade over it, ensuring the steak is well coated. Cover the dish and let the steak marinate in the refrigerator for at least 1 hour.
3. Preheat the Ninja Dual Zone Air Fryer to 200°C on zone 1 for 5 minutes.
4. Place the marinated steak in zone 1 of the air fryer and cook at 200°C for 5 minutes on each side, or until the steak reaches your desired level of doneness.
5. Once cooked, remove the steak from the air fryer and let it rest for a few minutes. Slice the steak against the grain into thin strips.
6. Garnish with fresh cilantro and serve with lime wedges. Carne asada can be enjoyed in tacos, burritos, or as a main dish with rice and beans.

Lebanese Kofta Kebabs

Serves: 4
Prep time: 30 minutes (+1 hour chilling time) / Cook time: 10 minutes

Ingredients:
- 500g ground lamb or beef
- 1 small onion, grated
- 2 cloves garlic, minced
- 2 tbsp fresh parsley, finely chopped
- 1 tbsp fresh mint, finely chopped
- 1 tsp ground cumin
- 1 tsp ground coriander
- 1/2 tsp ground cinnamon
- Salt and black pepper, to taste
- Vegetable oil, for brushing

Preparation instructions:
1. In a bowl, combine the ground lamb or beef, grated onion, minced garlic, chopped parsley, chopped mint, ground cumin, ground coriander, ground cinnamon, salt, and black pepper. Mix well until all the ingredients are evenly incorporated.
2. Shape the mixture into small, elongated kebab patties. Place the patties on a baking sheet and refrigerate for 1 hour to allow them to firm up.
3. Preheat the Ninja Dual Zone Air Fryer to 200°C on zone 1 for 5 minutes.
4. Brush the kofta kebabs with a little vegetable oil to prevent sticking. Place the kebabs in zone 1 of the air fryer and cook at 200°C for 10 minutes, turning halfway through cooking, or until the kebabs are cooked through and nicely browned.
5. Once cooked, remove the kofta kebabs from the air fryer and let them rest for a few minutes before serving. Serve with pita bread, tzatziki sauce, and a side of salad.

10 Vegan Katsu Curry

Serves: 4
Prep time: 30 minutes / Cook time: 15 minutes

Ingredients:
For the curry sauce:
- 1 tbsp vegetable oil
- 1 onion, finely chopped
- 2 cloves garlic, minced
- 2 carrots, diced
- 2 potatoes, diced
- 2 tbsp curry powder
- 1 tbsp plain flour
- 500ml vegetable broth
- 2 tbsp soy sauce
- 2 tbsp ketchup
- Salt and black pepper, to taste

For the breaded tofu:
- 400g firm tofu, drained and pressed
- 100g breadcrumbs
- 2 tbsp all-purpose flour
- 120ml plant-based milk
- 1 tbsp soy sauce
- 1/2 tsp garlic powder
- Vegetable oil, for frying

Preparation instructions:
1. In a frying pan, heat the vegetable oil over medium heat. Add the chopped onion and minced garlic, and sauté until translucent.
2. Add the diced carrots and potatoes to the frying pan, and cook for a few minutes until slightly softened.
3. Stir in the curry powder and plain flour, and cook for another minute to toast the spices.
4. Gradually add the vegetable broth, soy sauce, and ketchup to the pan, stirring well to combine. Bring the mixture to a simmer and let it cook until the vegetables are tender and the sauce has thickened. Season with salt and black pepper to taste.
5. Preheat the Ninja Dual Zone Air Fryer to

200°C on zone 1 for 5 minutes.
6. Cut the pressed tofu into thick slices or cubes.
7. In a shallow dish, combine the breadcrumbs, all-purpose flour, plant-based milk, soy sauce, and garlic powder to make the breading mixture.
8. Dip each tofu piece into the breading mixture, ensuring it is well coated on all sides.
9. Place the breaded tofu in zone 1 of the air fryer and cook at 200°C for 15 minutes, or until golden brown and crispy.
10. Once cooked, remove the tofu from the air fryer and let it cool slightly before serving.
11. Serve the crispy tofu over steamed rice, topped with the curry sauce. Optionally, garnish with chopped fresh parsley or cilantro. Enjoy your vegan katsu curry!

Peruvian Chicken

Serves: 4
Prep time: 15 minutes (+2 hours marinating time) / Cook time: 20 minutes

Ingredients:
- 800g chicken pieces (such as drumsticks or bone-in thighs)
- 3 cloves garlic, minced
- 2 tbsp lime juice
- 2 tbsp soy sauce
- 1 tbsp olive oil
- 1 tbsp paprika
- 1 tsp ground cumin
- 1 tsp dried oregano
- 1/2 tsp smoked paprika
- 1/4 tsp cayenne pepper (optional, for added spice)
- Salt and black pepper, to taste
- Fresh cilantro (coriander), chopped, for garnish
- Lime wedges, for serving

Preparation instructions:
1. In a bowl, combine the minced garlic, lime juice, soy sauce, olive oil, paprika, ground cumin, dried oregano, smoked paprika, cayenne pepper (if using), salt, and black pepper to make the marinade.
2. Place the chicken pieces in a shallow dish and pour the marinade over them, ensuring the chicken is well coated. Cover the dish and let the chicken marinate in the refrigerator for at least 2 hours, or overnight for even better flavour.
3. Preheat the Ninja Dual Zone Air Fryer to 200°C on zone 1 for 5 minutes.
4. Remove the chicken from the marinade, allowing any excess marinade to drip off.
5. Place the chicken pieces in zone 1 of the air fryer, making sure they are not overcrowded.
6. Air fry the chicken at 200°C for 20 minutes, or until the chicken is cooked through and the skin is crispy and golden brown. You may need to cook the chicken in batches depending on the size of your air fryer.
7. Once cooked, remove the chicken from the air fryer and let it rest for a few minutes before serving.
8. Garnish with freshly chopped cilantro and serve with lime wedges for squeezing over the chicken.
9. Peruvian chicken pairs well with steamed rice, roasted potatoes, or a fresh salad. Enjoy the flavorful and succulent Peruvian-style chicken!
10. Note: You can adjust the cooking time based on the size and thickness of the chicken pieces. Make sure to check for doneness by cutting into the thickest part of the chicken to ensure it is cooked through.

Chimichurri Steak

Serves: 4
Prep time: 10 minutes (+1 hour marinating time) / Cook time: 10 minutes

Ingredients:
- 600g steak (such as sirloin, ribeye, or flank),

about 2 cm thick
- 4 tbsp olive oil
- 3 tbsp red wine vinegar
- 2 cloves garlic, minced
- 2 tbsp chopped fresh parsley
- 1 tbsp chopped fresh oregano
- 1 tsp dried chilli flakes
- Salt and black pepper, to taste

Preparation instructions:
1. In a bowl, combine the olive oil, red wine vinegar, minced garlic, chopped parsley, chopped oregano, dried chilli flakes, salt, and black pepper to make the chimichurri marinade.
2. Place the steak in a shallow dish and pour the chimichurri marinade over it, making sure to coat the steak evenly. Cover the dish and let the steak marinate in the refrigerator for at least 1 hour.
3. Preheat the Ninja Dual Zone Air Fryer to 200°C on zone 1 for 5 minutes.
4. Remove the steak from the marinade and let any excess marinade drip off.
5. Place the steak in zone 1 of the air fryer and cook at 200°C for 8-10 minutes, or until the steak reaches your desired level of doneness, flipping halfway through.
6. Once cooked, remove the steak from the air fryer and let it rest for a few minutes before slicing. Serve with additional chimichurri sauce on top, if desired.

Vietnamese Lemongrass Pork

Serves: 4
Prep time: 15 minutes (+1 hour marinating time) / Cook time: 15 minutes

Ingredients:
- 600g pork tenderloin, thinly sliced
- 2 stalks lemongrass, white parts only, minced
- 4 cloves garlic, minced
- 2 tbsp fish sauce
- 2 tbsp soy sauce
- 1 tbsp vegetable oil
- 1 tbsp honey or brown sugar
- 1/2 tsp five-spice powder (optional)
- Salt and black pepper, to taste

Preparation instructions:
1. In a bowl, combine the minced lemongrass, minced garlic, fish sauce, soy sauce, vegetable oil, honey or brown sugar, five-spice powder (if using), salt, and black pepper to make the marinade.
2. Add the sliced pork tenderloin to the bowl and toss to coat the pork in the marinade. Cover the bowl and let the pork marinate in the refrigerator for at least 1 hour.
3. Preheat the Ninja Dual Zone Air Fryer to 200°C on zone 1 for 5 minutes.
4. Remove the pork from the marinade, allowing any excess marinade to drip off.
5. Place the pork slices in zone 1 of the air fryer and cook at 200°C for 12-15 minutes, or until the pork is cooked through and slightly caramelised, flipping halfway through.
6. Once cooked, remove the pork from the air fryer and let it rest for a few minutes before serving. Serve with steamed rice and fresh herbs, if desired.

Moroccan Chicken Tagine

Serves: 4
Prep time: 15 minutes (+2 hours marinating time) / Cook time: 30 minutes

Ingredients:
- 800g bone-in chicken pieces (such as thighs or drumsticks)
- 2 tbsp olive oil
- 1 onion, finely chopped
- 3 cloves garlic, minced
- 2 tsp ground cumin
- 2 tsp ground coriander
- 1 tsp ground turmeric
- 1/2 tsp ground cinnamon

- 1/4 tsp ground ginger
- 400g canned chopped tomatoes
- 200ml chicken broth
- 100g pitted green olives
- 2 preserved lemons, flesh discarded, rind thinly sliced
- Fresh cilantro (coriander), chopped, for garnish
- Salt and black pepper, to taste

Preparation instructions:
1. In a bowl, combine the olive oil, minced garlic, ground cumin, ground coriander, ground turmeric, ground cinnamon, and ground ginger to make a marinade.
2. Add the chicken pieces to the marinade, ensuring they are well coated. Cover the bowl and let the chicken marinate in the refrigerator for at least 2 hours, or overnight for better flavour.
3. Preheat the Ninja Dual Zone Air Fryer to 180°C on zone 1 for 5 minutes.
4. Heat a tablespoon of olive oil in a tagine or a deep frying pan over medium heat.
5. Add the chopped onion to the pan and sauté until softened and translucent.
6. Add the marinated chicken pieces to the pan and brown them on all sides.
7. Stir in the canned chopped tomatoes and chicken broth. Season with salt and black pepper to taste.
8. Cover the pan with a lid or foil and transfer it to zone 1 of the air fryer. Air fry at 180°C for 30 minutes or until the chicken is cooked through and tender.
9. Remove the pan from the air fryer and stir in the green olives and preserved lemon slices.
10. Garnish with freshly chopped cilantro and serve the Moroccan chicken tagine hot with couscous or crusty bread.

Mexican Street Corn

Serves: 4
Prep time: 10 minutes / Cook time: 15 minutes

Ingredients:
- 4 corn cobs, husks removed
- 2 tbsp mayonnaise
- 2 tbsp sour cream
- 2 tbsp fresh lime juice
- 50g grated Parmesan cheese
- 1/2 tsp chilli powder
- 1/4 tsp paprika
- Fresh cilantro (coriander), chopped, for garnish
- Lime wedges, for serving

Preparation instructions:
1. Preheat the Ninja Dual Zone Air Fryer to 200°C on zone 1 for 5 minutes.
2. Place the corn cobs in zone 1 of the air fryer and airfryer at 200°C for 15 minutes or until the corn is tender and lightly charred, turning occasionally for even cooking.
3. While the corn is cooking, in a small bowl, mix together the mayonnaise, sour cream, and lime juice to make the sauce.
4. In another bowl, combine the grated Parmesan cheese, chilli powder, and paprika.
5. Once the corn is cooked, remove it from the air fryer and brush each cob with the sauce mixture.
6. Sprinkle the cheese and spice mixture over the corn, coating each cob evenly.
7. Garnish with freshly chopped cilantro and serve the Mexican street corn hot with lime wedges for squeezing over the corn.

Paneer Tikka

Serves: 4
Prep time: 20 minutes (+1 hour marinating time) / Cook time: 12 minutes

Ingredients:
- 400g paneer, cut into cubes
- 1 bell pepper (capsicum), cut into cubes
- 1 red onion, cut into cubes
- 60ml plain yoghurt
- 1 tbsp ginger-garlic paste
- 1 tbsp lemon juice

- 1 tsp ground cumin
- 1 tsp ground coriander
- 1/2 tsp ground turmeric
- 1/2 tsp paprika
- 1/4 tsp garam masala
- Salt, to taste
- Fresh cilantro (coriander), chopped, for garnish
- Lemon wedges, for serving

Preparation instructions:

1. In a bowl, combine the plain yoghurt, ginger-garlic paste, lemon juice, ground cumin, ground coriander, ground turmeric, paprika, garam masala, and salt to make the marinade.
2. Add the paneer cubes, bell pepper, and red onion to the marinade, ensuring they are well coated. Cover the bowl and let the mixture marinate in the refrigerator for at least 1 hour.
3. Preheat the Ninja Dual Zone Air Fryer to 200°C on zone 1 for 5 minutes.
4. Thread the marinated paneer, bell pepper, and onion onto skewers.
5. Place the skewers in zone 1 of the air fryer and airfryer at 200°C for 12 minutes, or until the paneer is golden brown and the vegetables are slightly charred, turning the skewers halfway through cooking for even browning.
6. Once cooked, remove the skewers from the air fryer and garnish with freshly chopped cilantro.
7. Serve the paneer tikka hot with lemon wedges and mint chutney or yoghurt dip.

Vegan Quinoa and Sweet Potato Burgers

Serves: 4
Prep time: 20 minutes / Cook time: 20 minutes

Ingredients:
- 200g cooked quinoa
- 300g sweet potatoes, cooked and mashed
- 50g breadcrumbs
- 2 tbsp ground flaxseed + 6 tbsp water (flaxseed egg substitute)
- 1 small onion, finely chopped
- 2 cloves garlic, minced
- 2 tbsp chopped fresh parsley
- 1 tsp ground cumin
- 1/2 tsp smoked paprika
- Salt and black pepper, to taste
- 2 tbsp olive oil
- Burger buns and desired toppings, for serving

Preparation instructions:

1. In a small bowl, combine the ground flaxseed and water, and let it sit for 5 minutes to form a thick gel-like consistency (flaxseed egg substitute).
2. In a large mixing bowl, combine the cooked quinoa, mashed sweet potatoes, breadcrumbs, chopped onion, minced garlic, chopped parsley, ground cumin, smoked paprika, salt, and black pepper.
3. Add the flaxseed egg substitute to the mixture and stir until well combined. The mixture should be moist and hold together when shaped into patties. If needed, add more breadcrumbs to adjust the consistency.
4. Shape the mixture into burger patties of your desired size.
5. Preheat the Ninja Dual Zone Air Fryer to 180°C on zone 1 for 5 minutes.
6. Brush the olive oil onto the burgers to prevent sticking and place them in zone 1 of the air fryer.
7. Air fry the burgers at 180°C for 10 minutes on each side or until they are golden brown and crispy.
8. Once cooked, remove the burgers from the air fryer and assemble them on burger buns with your favourite toppings such as lettuce, tomato, onion, and vegan mayo.
9. Serve the vegan quinoa and sweet potato burgers hot and enjoy!

Vegan Shepherd's Pie

Serves: 4
Prep time: 20 minutes / Cook time: 40 minutes

Ingredients:

For the filling:
- 2 tbsp olive oil
- 1 onion, finely chopped
- 2 cloves garlic, minced
- 2 carrots, diced
- 2 celery stalks, diced
- 200g mushrooms, sliced
- 400g canned lentils, drained and rinsed
- 400g canned diced tomatoes
- 2 tbsp tomato paste
- 2 tsp dried thyme
- 1 tsp dried rosemary
- 1 tsp smoked paprika
- 250ml vegetable broth
- Salt and black pepper, to taste

For the mashed potato topping:
- 800g potatoes, peeled and cubed
- 60ml unsweetened almond milk or any plant-based milk
- 2 tbsp vegan butter or olive oil
- Salt and black pepper, to taste

Preparation instructions:

1. In a large frying pan, heat the olive oil over medium heat.
2. Add the chopped onion and minced garlic to the pan and sauté until the onion becomes translucent.
3. Add the diced carrots, diced celery, and sliced mushrooms to the pan. Cook for a few minutes until the vegetables start to soften.
4. Stir in the drained lentils, canned diced tomatoes, tomato paste, dried thyme, dried rosemary, smoked paprika, vegetable broth, salt, and black pepper. Simmer the mixture for 15-20 minutes, or until the flavours meld together and the liquid reduces slightly.
5. Preheat the Ninja Dual Zone Air Fryer to 180°C on zone 1 for 5 minutes.
6. While the filling is simmering, place the cubed potatoes in a saucepan and cover them with water. Bring the water to a boil and cook the potatoes until they are fork-tender. Drain the potatoes and return them to the saucepan.
7. Add the almond milk and vegan butter (or olive oil) to the saucepan with the cooked potatoes. Mash the potatoes until smooth and creamy. Season with salt and black pepper to taste.
8. Transfer the lentil and vegetable filling to an oven-safe dish. Spread the mashed potato topping over the filling, ensuring it covers the entire surface.
9. Place the dish in zone 1 of the air fryer and airfryer at 180°C for 20 minutes, or until the mashed potato topping forms a golden crust.
10. Once cooked, remove the vegan shepherd's pie from the air fryer and let it cool slightly before serving.
11. Serve the vegan shepherd's pie hot and enjoy a comforting and hearty meal.

Chickpea and Spinach Curry

Serves: 4
Prep time: 10 minutes / Cook time: 25 minutes

Ingredients:
- 2 tbsp vegetable oil
- 1 onion, finely chopped
- 3 cloves garlic, minced
- 1 tsp grated fresh ginger
- 1 tsp ground cumin
- 1 tsp ground coriander
- 1/2 tsp ground turmeric
- 1/2 tsp garam masala
- 1/4 tsp cayenne pepper (optional, for heat)
- 400g canned chickpeas, drained and rinsed
- 400g canned diced tomatoes

- 200ml coconut milk
- 100g baby spinach leaves
- Salt and black pepper, to taste
- Fresh cilantro (coriander), chopped, for garnish
- Cooked basmati rice or naan bread, for serving

Preparation instructions:

1. Preheat the Ninja Dual Zone Air Fryer to 180°C on zone 1 for 5 minutes.
2. In a large frying pan, heat the vegetable oil over medium heat.
3. Add the chopped onion to the pan and sauté until it becomes translucent.
4. Stir in the minced garlic and grated ginger, and cook for another minute.
5. Add the ground cumin, ground coriander, ground turmeric, garam masala, and cayenne pepper (if using) to the pan. Cook the spices for a minute to release their flavours.
6. Add the drained chickpeas, canned diced tomatoes, and coconut milk to the pan. Season with salt and black pepper to taste. Simmer the curry for 15-20 minutes, allowing the flavours to meld together.
7. Add the baby spinach leaves to the pan and stir them into the curry until wilted.
8. Place the pan in zone 1 of the air fryer and airfryer at 180°C for 5 minutes to further enhance the flavours.
9. Remove the pan from the air fryer and garnish the chickpea and spinach curry with freshly chopped cilantro.
10. Serve the curry hot with basmati rice or naan bread for a delicious and satisfying meal.

Air Fryer Veggie "Fried" Rice

Serves: 4
Prep time: 20 minutes / Cook time: 12-15 minutes

Ingredients:
- 240g cooked brown rice
- 1 tablespoon vegetable oil
- 1 onion, diced
- 2 garlic cloves, minced
- 1 tablespoon grated ginger
- 1 red bell pepper, diced
- 1 cup frozen peas and carrots
- 2 tablespoons soy sauce
- 1 teaspoon sesame oil
- Salt and pepper to taste
- 2 eggs, beaten (optional)

Preparation Instructions:

1. Preheat your air fryer to 400°F (200°C).
2. In a large skillet, heat the vegetable oil over medium-high heat.
3. Add the onion, garlic, and ginger and sauté until fragrant, about 2 minutes.
4. Add the red bell pepper and frozen peas and carrots and cook for another 5 minutes, until the vegetables are tender.
5. Add the cooked brown rice, soy sauce, sesame oil, salt, and pepper and stir until well combined.
6. Optional: Push the veggie rice mixture to one side of the skillet and add the beaten eggs to the other side. Scramble the eggs until cooked, then mix them into the veggie rice.
7. Transfer the veggie rice mixture to the air fryer basket, spreading it in an even layer.
8. Air fry for 5-8 minutes, until the rice is crispy and heated

Chapter 3: Fish and Seafood

Fish Tacos

Serves: 4
Prep time: 15 minutes / Cook time: 10 minutes

Ingredients:
For the fish:
- 400g white fish fillets (such as cod or haddock)
- 2 tbsp olive oil
- 1 tsp chilli powder
- 1/2 tsp ground cumin
- 1/2 tsp paprika
- Salt and black pepper, to taste

For the slaw:
- 150g shredded cabbage
- 1 carrot, grated
- 1/4 red onion, thinly sliced
- 2 tbsp mayonnaise
- 1 tbsp lime juice
- Salt and black pepper, to taste

For serving:
- 8 small flour tortillas
- Fresh cilantro (coriander) leaves, chopped
- Lime wedges

Preparation instructions:
1. Preheat the Ninja Dual Zone Air Fryer to 200°C on zone 1 for 5 minutes.
2. In a small bowl, combine the olive oil, chilli powder, ground cumin, paprika, salt, and black pepper to make a spice mixture.
3. Pat the fish fillets dry and brush them with the spice mixture on both sides.
4. Place the fish fillets in zone 1 of the air fryer and airfryer at 200°C for 8-10 minutes, or until the fish is cooked through and flakes easily with a fork.
5. While the fish is cooking, prepare the slaw by combining the shredded cabbage, grated carrot, thinly sliced red onion, mayonnaise, lime juice, salt, and black pepper in a bowl. Mix well to coat the vegetables.
6. Warm the flour tortillas according to package instructions.
7. Once the fish is cooked, remove it from the air fryer and let it cool slightly. Use a fork to break the fish into smaller pieces.
8. To assemble the tacos, place a spoonful of the slaw on a tortilla, top with some of the cooked fish, and sprinkle with chopped cilantro. Squeeze fresh lime juice over the filling.
9. Repeat with the remaining tortillas and filling.
10. Serve the fish tacos hot and enjoy a flavorful and refreshing meal.

Cajun Shrimp and Grits

Serves: 4
Prep time: 10 minutes / Cook time: 20 minutes

Ingredients:
For the shrimp:
- 400g large shrimp, peeled and deveined
- 2 tbsp Cajun seasoning
- 2 tbsp olive oil
- Salt and black pepper, to taste

For the grits:
- 200g quick-cooking grits
- 750ml water
- 60ml whole milk
- 30g unsalted butter
- Salt, to taste

For serving:
- 2 spring onions, thinly sliced
- Fresh parsley, chopped

Preparation instructions:
1. Preheat the Ninja Dual Zone Air Fryer to 200°C on zone 1 for 5 minutes.
2. In a bowl, toss the peeled and deveined

shrimp with Cajun seasoning, olive oil, salt, and black pepper until well coated.
3. Place the seasoned shrimp in zone 1 of the air fryer and airfryer at 200°C for 6-8 minutes, or until the shrimp are pink and cooked through.
4. While the shrimp are cooking, prepare the grits. In a saucepan, bring the water to a boil. Stir in the quick-cooking grits and reduce the heat to low. Cook the grits according to the package instructions, usually for about 5 minutes, stirring occasionally.
5. Once the grits are cooked, stir in the whole milk, unsalted butter, and salt to taste. Continue cooking for another 2-3 minutes until the grits are creamy and smooth.
6. Divide the cooked grits among 4 serving bowls.
7. Remove the cooked shrimp from the air fryer and place them on top of the grits.
8. Garnish with sliced spring onions and chopped parsley.
9. Serve the Cajun shrimp and grits hot, and enjoy the delightful combination of flavours and textures.

Crispy Calamari Rings

Serves: 4
Prep time: 15 minutes / Cook time: 10 minutes

Ingredients:
- 400g calamari rings
- 100g all-purpose flour
- 1 tsp paprika
- 1/2 tsp garlic powder
- Salt and black pepper, to taste
- 2 large eggs
- 2 tbsp milk
- Vegetable oil, for brushing

For serving:
- Lemon wedges
- Tartar sauce or marinara sauce

Preparation instructions:
1. Preheat the Ninja Dual Zone Air Fryer to 200°C on zone 1 for 5 minutes.
2. In a shallow bowl, mix together the all-purpose flour, paprika, garlic powder, salt, and black pepper.
3. In a separate bowl, whisk together the eggs and milk.
4. Dip each calamari ring into the egg mixture, allowing any excess to drip off, then coat it with the flour mixture. Shake off any excess flour.
5. Place the coated calamari rings in zone 1 of the air fryer and lightly brush them with vegetable oil.
6. Air fry the calamari rings at 200°C for 8-10 minutes, or until they turn golden brown and crispy.
7. Once cooked, remove the calamari rings from the air fryer and transfer them to a serving plate lined with paper towels to absorb any excess oil.
8. Serve the crispy calamari rings hot with lemon wedges and your choice of tartar sauce or marinara sauce for dipping.
9. Enjoy the deliciously crispy and tender calamari rings as a delightful appetiser or main course.
10. Note: Adjust the cooking time based on the size and thickness of the calamari rings for optimal results.

Garlic Butter Scallops

Serves: 4
Prep time: 10 minutes / Cook time: 6 minutes

Ingredients:
- 400g scallops
- 3 tbsp unsalted butter, melted
- 3 cloves garlic, minced
- 1 tbsp fresh parsley, chopped
- Salt and black pepper, to taste
- Lemon wedges, for serving

Preparation instructions:
1. Preheat the Ninja Dual Zone Air Fryer to 200°C on zone 1 for 5 minutes.
2. Pat the scallops dry using paper towels.
3. In a small bowl, combine the melted butter, minced garlic, chopped parsley, salt, and black pepper.
4. Dip each scallop into the garlic butter mixture, ensuring it's well coated.
5. Place the coated scallops in zone 1 of the air fryer in a single layer, making sure they are not overcrowded.
6. Air fry the scallops at 200°C for 4-6 minutes, depending on their size. Cook until they are opaque and slightly firm to the touch.
7. Once cooked, remove the scallops from the air fryer and transfer them to a serving plate.
8. Squeeze fresh lemon juice over the scallops for added brightness.
9. Serve the garlic butter scallops hot as an elegant appetiser or pair them with your favourite sides for a delicious main course.

Baja Fish Fillet

Serves: 4
Prep time: 15 minutes / Cook time: 12 minutes

Ingredients:
- 400g white fish fillets (such as cod or tilapia)
- 60ml lime juice
- 60g all-purpose flour
- 60g cornmeal
- 1 tsp paprika
- 1/2 tsp ground cumin
- Salt and black pepper, to taste
- 2 large eggs, beaten
- Vegetable oil, for brushing

For serving:
- Tortillas or lettuce leaves
- Sliced avocado
- Sliced red onion
- Chopped fresh cilantro (coriander)
- Lime wedges

Preparation instructions:
1. Preheat the Ninja Dual Zone Air Fryer to 200°C on zone 1 for 5 minutes.
2. Cut the white fish fillets into smaller, manageable pieces if needed.
3. Place the fish fillets in a shallow dish and pour the lime juice over them. Let them marinate for about 10 minutes.
4. In a separate shallow dish, combine the all-purpose flour, cornmeal, paprika, ground cumin, salt, and black pepper.
5. Dip each fish fillet into the beaten eggs, allowing any excess to drip off, then coat it with the flour mixture. Shake off any excess flour.
6. Place the coated fish fillets in zone 1 of the air fryer and lightly brush them with vegetable oil.
7. Air fry the fish fillets at 200°C for 10-12 minutes, or until they turn golden brown and crispy.
8. Once cooked, remove the fish fillets from the air fryer and let them cool slightly.
9. Serve the Baja fish fillets in tortillas or lettuce leaves, and garnish with sliced avocado, sliced red onion, chopped fresh cilantro, and a squeeze of fresh lime juice.
10. Enjoy the delicious and vibrant Baja-style fish fillets as a tasty taco filling or a refreshing seafood wrap.

Teriyaki Glazed Salmon

Serves: 4
Prep time: 10 minutes / Cook time: 12 minutes

Ingredients:
- 4 salmon fillets (about 150g each)
- 4 tbsp teriyaki sauce
- 2 tbsp honey
- 1 tbsp soy sauce

- 1 tbsp rice vinegar
- 1/2 tsp grated fresh ginger
- Sesame seeds, for garnish
- Sliced spring onions, for garnish

Preparation instructions:
1. Preheat the Ninja Dual Zone Air Fryer to 200°C on zone 1 for 5 minutes.
2. In a small bowl, whisk together the teriyaki sauce, honey, soy sauce, rice vinegar, and grated fresh ginger to make the glaze.
3. Place the salmon fillets in zone 1 of the air fryer and brush them generously with the teriyaki glaze.
4. Air fry the salmon fillets at 200°C for 10-12 minutes, or until they are cooked to your desired doneness.
5. Once cooked, remove the salmon fillets from the air fryer and let them rest for a few minutes.
6. Sprinkle sesame seeds and sliced spring onions over the salmon fillets for garnish.
7. Serve the teriyaki glazed salmon hot with steamed rice or your favourite side dishes for a satisfying and flavorful meal.

Mediterranean Grilled Octopus

Serves: 4
Prep time: 15 minutes / Cook time: 20 minutes

Ingredients:
- 500g octopus tentacles, cleaned and tenderised
- 2 tbsp olive oil
- 2 cloves garlic, minced
- 1 tsp dried oregano
- 1/2 tsp paprika
- Salt and black pepper, to taste
- Lemon wedges, for serving

Preparation instructions:
1. Preheat the Ninja Dual Zone Air Fryer to 200°C on zone 1 for 5 minutes.
2. In a bowl, combine the olive oil, minced garlic, dried oregano, paprika, salt, and black pepper.
3. Add the cleaned and tenderised octopus tentacles to the bowl and toss them in the marinade until well coated.
4. Place the octopus tentacles in zone 1 of the air fryer in a single layer.
5. Air fry the octopus tentacles at 200°C for 18-20 minutes, or until they are tender and slightly charred.
6. Once cooked, remove the octopus tentacles from the air fryer and let them cool for a few minutes.
7. Slice the octopus tentacles into bite-sized pieces.
8. Serve the Mediterranean grilled octopus warm with lemon wedges for squeezing over the top. It pairs well with a fresh salad or crusty bread.

Jamaican Brown Stew Fish

Serves: 4
Prep time: 15 minutes / Cook time: 20 minutes

Ingredients:
- 4 white fish fillets (such as snapper or tilapia)
- 2 tbsp all-purpose flour
- 1 tsp paprika
- 1/2 tsp dried thyme
- 1/2 tsp ground allspice
- Salt and black pepper, to taste
- 2 tbsp vegetable oil
- 1 onion, sliced
- 2 cloves garlic, minced
- 1 bell pepper, sliced
- 1 carrot, sliced
- 2 tomatoes, diced
- 250ml vegetable or fish stock
- 2 tbsp soy sauce
- 1 tbsp Worcestershire sauce
- 1 tbsp brown sugar

- Fresh parsley, chopped, for garnish

Preparation instructions:
1. Preheat the Ninja Dual Zone Air Fryer to 200°C on zone 1 for 5 minutes.
2. In a shallow dish, combine the all-purpose flour, paprika, dried thyme, ground allspice, salt, and black pepper.
3. Pat the fish fillets dry using paper towels, then coat them with the flour mixture, shaking off any excess.
4. Place the coated fish fillets in zone 1 of the air fryer and lightly brush them with vegetable oil.
5. Air fry the fish fillets at 200°C for 10-12 minutes, or until they turn golden brown and crispy. Remove them from the air fryer and set aside.
6. In a large saucepan or skillet, heat the vegetable oil over medium heat. Add the sliced onion, minced garlic, bell pepper, and carrot. Sauté for about 5 minutes, or until the vegetables are softened.
7. Stir in the diced tomatoes, vegetable or fish stock, soy sauce, Worcestershire sauce, and brown sugar. Bring the mixture to a simmer and cook for about 5 minutes, allowing the flavours to meld.
8. Add the air-fried fish fillets to the saucepan or skillet, gently spooning the stew sauce over them. Simmer for another 5 minutes to ensure the fish is cooked through and absorbs the flavours.
9. Serve the Jamaican brown stew fish hot, garnished with freshly chopped parsley. It goes well with steamed rice and plantains for a traditional Jamaican meal.

Spicy Shrimp and Broccoli

Serves: 4
Prep time: 15 minutes / Cook time: 10 minutes

Ingredients:
- 400g shrimp, peeled and deveined
- 2 tbsp soy sauce
- 2 tbsp Sriracha sauce
- 1 tbsp honey
- 2 cloves garlic, minced
- 1 tsp grated fresh ginger
- 2 tbsp vegetable oil
- 1 broccoli head, cut into florets
- Salt and black pepper, to taste
- Sliced spring onions, for garnish

Preparation instructions:
1. Preheat the Ninja Dual Zone Air Fryer to 200°C on zone 1 for 5 minutes.
2. In a bowl, whisk together the soy sauce, Sriracha sauce, honey, minced garlic, and grated fresh ginger to create the spicy sauce.
3. Add the peeled and deveined shrimp to the bowl and toss them in the spicy sauce until well coated.
4. In zone 2 of the air fryer, add the broccoli florets, drizzle with vegetable oil, and season with salt and black pepper. Toss to coat evenly.
5. Place the shrimp in zone 1 and the broccoli in zone 2.
6. Air fry at 200°C for 8-10 minutes, or until the shrimp are pink and cooked through, and the broccoli is tender-crisp.
7. Once cooked, remove the shrimp and broccoli from the air fryer and transfer them to a serving dish.
8. Garnish with sliced spring onions for an added pop of freshness.
9. Serve the spicy shrimp and broccoli hot over steamed rice or noodles, and enjoy the bold and vibrant flavours.

Thai Sweet Chili Salmon

Serves: 4
Prep time: 10 minutes / Cook time: 12 minutes

Ingredients:
- 4 salmon fillets (about 150g each)
- 4 tbsp Thai sweet chilli sauce
- 2 tbsp soy sauce
- 2 tbsp lime juice
- 1 tbsp vegetable oil
- 1 tbsp chopped fresh cilantro (coriander)
- Sesame seeds, for garnish
- Sliced spring onions, for garnish

Preparation instructions:
1. Preheat the Ninja Dual Zone Air Fryer to 200°C on zone 1 for 5 minutes.
2. In a small bowl, whisk together the Thai sweet chilli sauce, soy sauce, lime juice, vegetable oil, and chopped fresh cilantro.
3. Place the salmon fillets in zone 1 of the air fryer and brush them generously with the Thai sweet chilli sauce mixture.
4. Air fry the salmon fillets at 200°C for 10-12 minutes, or until they are cooked to your desired doneness.
5. Once cooked, remove the salmon fillets from the air fryer and let them rest for a few minutes.
6. Sprinkle sesame seeds and sliced spring onions over the salmon fillets for garnish.
7. Serve the Thai sweet chilli salmon hot with steamed rice and stir-fried vegetables for a delightful Asian-inspired meal.

Lemon Garlic Shrimp

Serves: 4
Prep time: 10 minutes / Cook time: 6 minutes

Ingredients:
- 400g shrimp, peeled and deveined
- 2 tbsp olive oil
- 3 cloves garlic, minced
- Zest of 1 lemon
- Juice of 1 lemon
- 1 tbsp chopped fresh parsley
- Salt and black pepper, to taste

Preparation instructions:
1. Preheat the Ninja Dual Zone Air Fryer to 200°C on zone 1 for 5 minutes.
2. In a bowl, combine the peeled and deveined shrimp, olive oil, minced garlic, lemon zest, lemon juice, chopped fresh parsley, salt, and black pepper. Toss until the shrimp are well coated.
3. Place the shrimp in zone 1 of the air fryer in a single layer.
4. Air fry the shrimp at 200°C for 5-6 minutes, or until they are pink and cooked through.
5. Once cooked, remove the shrimp from the air fryer and let them rest for a minute.
6. Serve the lemon garlic shrimp hot, with a squeeze of fresh lemon juice over the top. It pairs well with rice, pasta, or a fresh green salad for a light and zesty meal.

Sesame Ginger Tuna

Serves: 4
Prep time: 10 minutes / Cook time: 6 minutes

Ingredients:
- 4 tuna steaks (about 150g each)
- 2 tbsp soy sauce
- 1 tbsp sesame oil
- 1 tbsp grated fresh ginger
- 1 tbsp honey
- 1 tbsp sesame seeds
- Sliced spring onions, for garnish

Preparation instructions:
1. Preheat the Ninja Dual Zone Air Fryer to 200°C on zone 1 for 5 minutes.
2. In a bowl, whisk together the soy sauce, sesame oil, grated fresh ginger, and honey to

create the marinade.

3. Place the tuna steaks in the marinade and let them marinate for about 5 minutes, turning once.
4. Sprinkle sesame seeds over the tuna steaks, pressing them lightly to adhere.
5. Place the tuna steaks in zone 1 of the air fryer and lightly brush them with any remaining marinade.
6. Air fry the tuna steaks at 200°C for 3-4 minutes on each side, or until they are cooked to your desired doneness.
7. Once cooked, remove the tuna steaks from the air fryer and let them rest for a minute.
8. Garnish with sliced spring onions for added freshness and presentation.
9. Serve the sesame ginger tuna hot, accompanied by steamed rice or a refreshing salad, for a satisfying and flavorful seafood dish.

Cajun Salmon Patties

Serves: 4
Prep time: 15 minutes / Cook time: 10 minutes

Ingredients:
- 400g canned salmon, drained and flaked
- 60g breadcrumbs
- 60g mayonnaise
- 1 egg, beaten
- 2 green onions, finely chopped
- 1 celery stalk, finely chopped
- 1/2 red bell pepper, finely chopped
- 1 tbsp Cajun seasoning
- 1 tbsp lemon juice
- Salt and black pepper, to taste
- Vegetable oil, for frying

Preparation instructions:
1. Preheat the Ninja Dual Zone Air Fryer to 200°C on zone 1 for 5 minutes.
2. In a bowl, combine the canned salmon, breadcrumbs, mayonnaise, beaten egg, finely chopped green onions, celery, red bell pepper, Cajun seasoning, lemon juice, salt, and black pepper. Mix well until all the ingredients are evenly incorporated.
3. Form the salmon mixture into patties of your desired size.
4. Place the salmon patties in zone 1 of the air fryer and lightly brush them with vegetable oil.
5. Air fry the salmon patties at 200°C for 8-10 minutes, flipping them halfway through, or until they are golden brown and heated through.
6. Once cooked, remove the salmon patties from the air fryer and let them cool slightly before serving.
7. Serve the Cajun salmon patties hot as a main dish or in burger buns with your favourite condiments and toppings.

Brazilian Moqueca de Peixe (Fish Stew)

Serves: 4
Prep time: 20 minutes / Cook time: 30 minutes

Ingredients:
- 400g white fish fillets (such as snapper or cod), cut into chunks
- 1 onion, sliced
- 2 cloves garlic, minced
- 1 red bell pepper, sliced
- 1 yellow bell pepper, sliced
- 1 can (400g) diced tomatoes
- 200ml coconut milk
- 2 tbsp tomato paste
- 2 tbsp lime juice
- 2 tbsp chopped fresh cilantro (coriander)
- 2 tbsp olive oil
- 1 tsp paprika
- 1/2 tsp ground cumin

- 1/2 tsp ground turmeric
- Salt and black pepper, to taste
- Cooked rice, for serving
- Lime wedges, for serving

Preparation instructions:

1. Preheat the Ninja Dual Zone Air Fryer to 180°C on zone 1 for 5 minutes.
2. In a large saucepan or skillet, heat the olive oil over medium heat. Add the sliced onion, minced garlic, and bell peppers. Sauté for about 5 minutes, or until the vegetables are softened.
3. Stir in the paprika, ground cumin, and ground turmeric. Cook for another minute to toast the spices and release their flavours.
4. Add the diced tomatoes, coconut milk, tomato paste, lime juice, salt, and black pepper to the saucepan or skillet. Bring the mixture to a simmer and cook for 10 minutes, allowing the flavours to meld.
5. Season the fish fillet chunks with salt and black pepper.
6. Place the fish fillet chunks in zone 1 of the air fryer and pour the simmered vegetable and tomato mixture over them.
7. Air fry the fish stew at 180°C for 15-18 minutes, or until the fish is cooked through and flakes easily.
8. Once cooked, remove the fish stew from the air fryer and garnish with chopped fresh cilantro.
9. Serve the Brazilian Moqueca de Peixe hot over cooked rice, with lime wedges on the side. Enjoy the rich and vibrant flavours of this traditional Brazilian fish stew.

Spanish Paella with Seafood

Serves: 4
Prep time: 15 minutes / Cook time: 25 minutes

Ingredients:

- 250g paella rice (such as Arborio or Valencia)
- 400ml fish or vegetable stock
- 200ml white wine
- 1 onion, chopped
- 2 cloves garlic, minced
- 1 red bell pepper, sliced
- 100g frozen peas
- 200g mixed seafood (such as shrimp, mussels, and calamari)
- 2 tbsp olive oil
- 1 tsp smoked paprika
- 1/2 tsp saffron threads
- Salt and black pepper, to taste
- Lemon wedges, for serving
- Chopped fresh parsley, for garnish

Preparation instructions:

1. Preheat the Ninja Dual Zone Air Fryer to 180°C on zone 1 for 5 minutes.
2. In a large saucepan or skillet, heat the olive oil over medium heat. Add the chopped onion and minced garlic, and sauté for about 5 minutes, or until the onion is translucent.
3. Stir in the sliced red bell pepper, frozen peas, smoked paprika, and saffron threads. Cook for another minute to toast the spices and release their flavours.
4. Add the paella rice to the saucepan or skillet and stir to coat it with the onion and spice mixture.
5. Pour in the white wine and let it simmer for a minute or two to reduce slightly.
6. Gradually add the fish or vegetable stock, stirring occasionally, and simmer for about 15-18 minutes, or until the rice is tender and has absorbed most of the liquid. Add more

stock if needed.
7. Season the mixed seafood with salt and black pepper.
8. Place the mixed seafood in zone 1 of the air fryer and cook at 180°C for 5-7 minutes, or until the seafood is cooked through.
9. Once the rice is cooked, remove the saucepan or skillet from the heat and gently fold in the cooked seafood.
10. Serve the Spanish paella with seafood hot, garnished with chopped fresh parsley and accompanied by lemon wedges for squeezing over the top. It's a delightful and satisfying dish that showcases the flavours of the Mediterranean.

Cajun Shrimp Alfredo

Serves: 4
Prep time: 10 minutes / Cook time: 15 minutes

Ingredients:
- 400g linguine or fettuccine pasta
- 400g shrimp, peeled and deveined
- 2 tbsp Cajun seasoning
- 4 tbsp butter
- 4 cloves garlic, minced
- 250ml heavy cream
- 50g grated Parmesan cheese
- Salt and black pepper, to taste
- Chopped fresh parsley, for garnish

Preparation instructions:
1. Preheat the Ninja Dual Zone Air Fryer to 200°C on zone 1 for 5 minutes.
2. Cook the pasta according to the package instructions until al dente. Drain and set aside.
3. In a bowl, toss the peeled and deveined shrimp with Cajun seasoning until well coated.
4. Place the seasoned shrimp in zone 1 of the air fryer and cook at 200°C for 5-6 minutes, or until the shrimp are pink and cooked through.
5. In a large skillet, melt the butter over medium heat. Add the minced garlic and sauté for about a minute, until fragrant.
6. Stir in the heavy cream and bring the mixture to a simmer. Cook for a few minutes until the sauce thickens slightly.
7. Remove the skillet from the heat and stir in the grated Parmesan cheese until melted and smooth. Season with salt and black pepper to taste.
8. Add the cooked pasta to the skillet and toss to coat it with the creamy Alfredo sauce.
9. Place the Cajun shrimp on top of the pasta and garnish with chopped fresh parsley.
10. Serve the Cajun shrimp Alfredo hot, and enjoy the creamy and flavorful combination of Cajun-spiced shrimp and rich Alfredo sauce.

Sriracha Honey Glazed Salmon

Serves: 4
Prep time: 10 minutes / Cook time: 12 minutes

Ingredients:
- 4 salmon fillets (about 150g each)
- 2 tbsp sriracha sauce
- 2 tbsp honey
- 2 tbsp soy sauce
- 2 cloves garlic, minced
- 1 tbsp grated fresh ginger
- 1 tbsp vegetable oil
- Sesame seeds, for garnish
- Sliced spring onions, for garnish

Preparation instructions:
1. Preheat the Ninja Dual Zone Air Fryer to 200°C on zone 1 for 5 minutes.
2. In a bowl, whisk together the sriracha sauce, honey, soy sauce, minced garlic, grated fresh ginger, and vegetable oil to create the glaze.

3. Place the salmon fillets in zone 1 of the air fryer and brush them generously with the sriracha honey glaze.
4. Air fry the salmon fillets at 200°C for 10-12 minutes, or until they are cooked to your desired doneness.
5. Once cooked, remove the salmon fillets from the air fryer and let them rest for a minute.
6. Garnish the salmon fillets with sesame seeds and sliced spring onions for added flavour and presentation.
7. Serve the sriracha honey glazed salmon hot, accompanied by steamed rice or roasted vegetables, for a sweet and spicy seafood delight.

Singaporean Chili Crab

Serves: 4
Prep time: 20 minutes / Cook time: 15 minutes

Ingredients:
- 2 whole crabs (about 1 kg), cleaned and quartered
- 4 tbsp vegetable oil
- 4 cloves garlic, minced
- 2 red chilli peppers, sliced
- 2 tbsp tomato paste
- 2 tbsp sweet chilli sauce
- 2 tbsp soy sauce
- 2 tbsp oyster sauce
- 1 tbsp rice vinegar
- 1 tbsp sugar
- 120 ml water
- 2 spring onions, chopped (for garnish)
- Coriander leaves, for garnish

Preparation instructions:
1. Preheat the Ninja Dual Zone Air Fryer to 180°C on zone 1 for 5 minutes.
2. In a large skillet or wok, heat the vegetable oil over medium heat. Add the minced garlic and sliced red chilli peppers, and sauté for about a minute until fragrant.
3. Stir in the tomato paste, sweet chilli sauce, soy sauce, oyster sauce, rice vinegar, sugar, and water. Mix well to combine all the ingredients.
4. Place the crab quarters in zone 1 of the air fryer and pour the chilli sauce mixture over them.
5. Air fry the chilli crab at 180°C for 12-15 minutes, or until the crab is cooked through and the sauce has thickened slightly.
6. Once cooked, remove the chilli crab from the air fryer and transfer it to a serving dish.
7. Garnish the chilli crab with chopped spring onions and coriander leaves for added freshness and presentation.
8. Serve the Singaporean chilli crab hot with steamed rice or crusty bread to soak up the delicious sauce. Enjoy the bold and spicy flavours of this iconic seafood dish.

Chapter 4: Poultry & Meat Recipes

Argentinian Chimichurri Chicken

Serves: 4
Prep time: 15 minutes / Cook time: 15 minutes

Ingredients:
- 4 chicken breasts (about 600g), boneless and skinless
- 4 tbsp olive oil
- 4 cloves garlic, minced
- 2 tbsp red wine vinegar
- 2 tbsp fresh lemon juice
- 2 tbsp chopped fresh parsley
- 2 tbsp chopped fresh cilantro
- 1 tsp dried oregano
- 1/2 tsp red pepper flakes
- Salt and black pepper, to taste

Preparation instructions:
1. Preheat the Ninja Dual Zone Air Fryer to 200°C on zone 1 for 5 minutes.
2. In a bowl, combine the olive oil, minced garlic, red wine vinegar, lemon juice, chopped parsley, chopped cilantro, dried oregano, red pepper flakes, salt, and black pepper to make the chimichurri marinade.
3. Place the chicken breasts in a shallow dish and pour the chimichurri marinade over them, ensuring they are well coated. Let marinate for 10 minutes.
4. Place the marinated chicken breasts in zone 1 of the air fryer and cook at 200°C for 12-15 minutes, or until the chicken is cooked through and no longer pink in the centre.
5. Once cooked, remove the chicken breasts from the air fryer and let them rest for a few minutes.
6. Serve the Argentinian chimichurri chicken hot, garnished with extra chopped parsley and cilantro, alongside your choice of sides such as roasted potatoes or a fresh salad. Enjoy the vibrant flavours of the chimichurri sauce paired with tender, juicy chicken.

Turkish Kofta Kebabs

Serves: 4
Prep time: 15 minutes / Cook time: 12 minutes

Ingredients:
- 500g ground lamb or beef
- 1 small onion, grated
- 2 cloves garlic, minced
- 2 tbsp chopped fresh parsley
- 1 tsp ground cumin
- 1 tsp ground coriander
- 1/2 tsp paprika
- 1/4 tsp cinnamon
- Salt and black pepper, to taste
- Olive oil, for brushing

Preparation instructions:
1. Preheat the Ninja Dual Zone Air Fryer to 200°C on zone 1 for 5 minutes.
2. In a bowl, combine the ground lamb or beef, grated onion, minced garlic, chopped parsley, ground cumin, ground coriander, paprika, cinnamon, salt, and black pepper. Mix well until all the ingredients are evenly incorporated.
3. Divide the mixture into 8 portions and shape each portion into a long kebab shape.
4. Place the kofta kebabs in zone 1 of the air fryer and brush them with olive oil.
5. Air fry the kofta kebabs at 200°C for 10-12 minutes, or until they are cooked through and nicely browned on the outside.
6. Once cooked, remove the kofta kebabs from

the air fryer and let them rest for a minute.
7. Serve the Turkish kofta kebabs hot, accompanied by flatbread, tzatziki sauce, and a fresh salad for a delicious and satisfying meal.

Brazilian Picanha Steak

Serves: 4
Prep time: 10 minutes / Cook time: 15 minutes

Ingredients:
- 800g picanha steak (also known as rump cap or sirloin cap)
- 2 tbsp coarse sea salt
- 1 tbsp vegetable oil
- Chimichurri sauce, for serving (optional)

Preparation instructions:
1. Preheat the Ninja Dual Zone Air Fryer to 200°C on zone 1 for 5 minutes.
2. Sprinkle the coarse sea salt evenly over the picanha steak, pressing it gently into the meat.
3. Place the picanha steak in zone 1 of the air fryer and drizzle it with vegetable oil.
4. Air fry the picanha steak at 200°C for 12-15 minutes, flipping it halfway through the cooking time, or until it reaches your desired level of doneness.
5. Once cooked, remove the picanha steak from the air fryer and let it rest for a few minutes.
6. Slice the picanha steak against the grain and serve it hot. Optionally, you can serve it with chimichurri sauce for added flavour and freshness.

Greek Souvlaki Pork Skewers

Serves: 4
Prep time: 15 minutes (+ marinating time) / Cook time: 12 minutes

Ingredients:
- 500g pork tenderloin, cut into cubes
- 2 tbsp olive oil
- 2 tbsp fresh lemon juice
- 2 cloves garlic, minced
- 1 tsp dried oregano
- 1/2 tsp dried thyme
- Salt and black pepper, to taste
- Tzatziki sauce, for serving

Preparation instructions:
1. Preheat the Ninja Dual Zone Air Fryer to 200°C on zone 1 for 5 minutes.
2. In a bowl, combine the olive oil, lemon juice, minced garlic, dried oregano, dried thyme, salt, and black pepper to make the marinade.
3. Add the pork cubes to the marinade and toss to coat them evenly. Let the pork marinate in the refrigerator for at least 30 minutes, or up to 4 hours for more flavour.
4. Thread the marinated pork cubes onto skewers, leaving a small gap between each cube.
5. Place the pork skewers in zone 1 of the air fryer and cook at 200°C for 10-12 minutes, or until the pork is cooked through and slightly charred on the edges.
6. Once cooked, remove the pork skewers from the air fryer and let them rest for a minute.
7. Serve the Greek souvlaki pork skewers hot, accompanied by tzatziki sauce and your choice of sides such as pita bread, salad, or roasted vegetables.

Italian Breaded Chicken Cutlets

Serves: 4
Prep time: 15 minutes / Cook time: 10 minutes

Ingredients:
- 4 boneless, skinless chicken breasts (about 600g)
- 60g all-purpose flour
- 2 large eggs

- 120g breadcrumbs
- 40g grated Parmesan cheese
- 1 tsp dried oregano
- 1 tsp dried basil
- 1/2 tsp garlic powder
- 1/2 tsp onion powder
- Salt and black pepper, to taste
- Olive oil, for brushing

Preparation instructions:

1. Preheat the Ninja Dual Zone Air Fryer to 200°C on zone 1 for 5 minutes.
2. Place the all-purpose flour in a shallow dish. In another shallow dish, beat the eggs. In a third shallow dish, combine the breadcrumbs, grated Parmesan cheese, dried oregano, dried basil, garlic powder, onion powder, salt, and black pepper.
3. Dip each chicken breast into the flour, shaking off any excess. Then dip it into the beaten eggs, allowing any excess to drip off. Finally, coat the chicken breast with the breadcrumb mixture, pressing gently to adhere the crumbs.
4. Place the breaded chicken cutlets in zone 1 of the air fryer and brush them lightly with olive oil.
5. Air fry the chicken cutlets at 200°C for 8-10 minutes, or until they are cooked through and golden brown.
6. Once cooked, remove the chicken cutlets from the air fryer and let them rest for a few minutes.
7. Serve the Italian breaded chicken cutlets hot, alongside a fresh salad or your favourite side dishes.

Chinese Honey Sesame Chicken

Serves: 4
Prep time: 15 minutes / Cook time: 12 minutes

Ingredients:

- 500g boneless, skinless chicken thighs, cut into bite-sized pieces
- 3 tbsp soy sauce
- 2 tbsp honey
- 2 tbsp hoisin sauce
- 1 tbsp rice vinegar
- 2 cloves garlic, minced
- 1 tsp grated fresh ginger
- 1 tsp sesame oil
- 1 tbsp cornstarch
- 2 tbsp water
- 1 tbsp sesame seeds, for garnish
- Sliced green onions, for garnish

Preparation instructions:

1. Preheat the Ninja Dual Zone Air Fryer to 200°C on zone 1 for 5 minutes.
2. In a bowl, combine the soy sauce, honey, hoisin sauce, rice vinegar, minced garlic, grated ginger, and sesame oil to make the sauce.
3. Place the chicken thigh pieces in a separate bowl and pour half of the sauce over the chicken, reserving the remaining sauce for later. Toss the chicken in the sauce to coat it evenly.
4. Place the chicken pieces in zone 1 of the air fryer, making sure they are in a single layer and not overcrowded.
5. Air fry the chicken at 200°C for 10-12 minutes, shaking the basket or flipping the chicken halfway through the cooking time, or until the chicken is cooked through and nicely browned.
6. While the chicken is cooking, in a small bowl, whisk together the cornstarch and

water to make a slurry.
7. In a saucepan, heat the reserved sauce over medium heat. Once it simmers, whisk in the cornstarch slurry and continue cooking until the sauce thickens.
8. Once cooked, remove the chicken from the air fryer and toss it with the thickened sauce to coat it evenly.
9. Serve the Chinese honey sesame chicken hot, garnished with sesame seeds and sliced green onions. It pairs well with steamed rice and stir-fried vegetables.

Moroccan Lamb Meatballs

Serves: 4
Prep time: 15 minutes / Cook time: 15 minutes

Ingredients:
- 500g ground lamb
- 1 small onion, finely chopped
- 2 cloves garlic, minced
- 2 tbsp chopped fresh parsley
- 1 tsp ground cumin
- 1 tsp ground coriander
- 1/2 tsp ground cinnamon
- 1/2 tsp paprika
- 1/4 tsp ground ginger
- 1/4 tsp cayenne pepper (optional)
- Salt and black pepper, to taste
- Olive oil, for brushing

Preparation instructions:
1. Preheat the Ninja Dual Zone Air Fryer to 200°C on zone 1 for 5 minutes.
2. In a bowl, combine the ground lamb, finely chopped onion, minced garlic, chopped parsley, ground cumin, ground coriander, ground cinnamon, paprika, ground ginger, cayenne pepper (if using), salt, and black pepper. Mix well until all the ingredients are evenly incorporated.
3. Shape the lamb mixture into small meatballs, about 1-inch in diameter.
4. Place the lamb meatballs in zone 1 of the air fryer and brush them lightly with olive oil.
5. Air fry the meatballs at 200°C for 12-15 minutes, or until they are cooked through and nicely browned on the outside.
6. Once cooked, remove the lamb meatballs from the air fryer and let them rest for a minute.
7. Serve the Moroccan lamb meatballs hot, accompanied by couscous or rice, and a side of yoghurt sauce or mint chutney. Enjoy the aromatic and flavorful taste of these delightful meatballs.

Thai Basil Pork Stir Fry

Serves: 4
Prep time: 15 minutes / Cook time: 10 minutes

Ingredients:
- 500g pork tenderloin, thinly sliced
- 2 tbsp vegetable oil
- 4 cloves garlic, minced
- 2 red chilies, sliced
- 1 bell pepper, thinly sliced
- 1 onion, thinly sliced
- 200g fresh Thai basil leaves
- 2 tbsp soy sauce
- 1 tbsp oyster sauce
- 1 tbsp fish sauce
- 1 tbsp brown sugar
- Lime wedges, for serving

Preparation instructions:
1. Preheat the Ninja Dual Zone Air Fryer to 200°C on zone 1 for 5 minutes.
2. In a bowl, combine the soy sauce, oyster sauce, fish sauce, and brown sugar to make the sauce. Set aside.
3. Place the pork slices in a separate bowl and season them with salt and black pepper.
4. In zone 1 of the air fryer, heat the vegetable

oil for a minute.
5. Add the minced garlic and sliced red chilies to the air fryer and cook for about 1 minute, or until fragrant.
6. Add the seasoned pork slices to the air fryer and cook for 3-4 minutes, or until they are browned and cooked through.
7. Push the cooked pork to one side of the air fryer and add the bell pepper and onion slices. Stir fry them for 2-3 minutes, or until they are slightly softened.
8. Pour the sauce over the ingredients in the air fryer and stir everything together to coat it evenly.
9. Add the fresh Thai basil leaves to the air fryer and stir fry for an additional minute, until the basil wilts.
10. Once cooked, remove the Thai basil pork stir fry from the air fryer and let it rest for a minute.
11. Serve the stir fry hot, accompanied by steamed rice and lime wedges for squeezing over the dish. Enjoy the bold and aromatic flavours of this Thai-inspired pork stir fry.

Jamaican Beef Patty

Serves: 4
Prep time: 30 minutes / Cook time: 20 minutes

Ingredients:

For the pastry:
- 250g all-purpose flour
- 1/2 tsp turmeric powder (optional, for colour)
- 1/2 tsp salt
- 115g unsalted butter, cold and cubed
- 60ml ice water

For the filling:
- 300g ground beef
- 1 small onion, finely chopped
- 1 clove garlic, minced
- 1 small carrot, finely grated
- 1 small potato, finely grated
- 2 tbsp vegetable oil
- 1 tsp curry powder
- 1/2 tsp dried thyme
- 1/4 tsp ground allspice
- Salt and black pepper, to taste
- 60ml beef or vegetable broth

Preparation instructions:
1. Preheat the Ninja Dual Zone Air Fryer to 180°C on zone 1 for 5 minutes.
2. In a large bowl, combine the all-purpose flour, turmeric powder (if using), and salt for the pastry.
3. Add the cold cubed butter to the flour mixture and use your fingers or a pastry cutter to cut the butter into the flour until it resembles coarse crumbs.
4. Gradually add the ice water, a few tablespoons at a time, and mix until the dough comes together. Be careful not to overmix.
5. Shape the dough into a disk, wrap it in plastic wrap, and refrigerate for at least 15 minutes.
6. While the dough is chilling, prepare the filling. In a pan, heat the vegetable oil over medium heat.
7. Add the chopped onion and minced garlic to the pan and sauté for 2-3 minutes, until they are softened and aromatic.
8. Add the ground beef to the pan and cook until it is browned and cooked through.
9. Stir in the grated carrot, grated potato, curry powder, dried thyme, ground allspice, salt, black pepper, and beef or vegetable broth. Cook for an additional 5 minutes, or until the vegetables are tender and the flavours have melded together.
10. Remove the filling from the heat and let it cool slightly.
11. Remove the chilled dough from the refrigerator and roll it out on a floured

surface to a thickness of about 3-4 mm.
12. Use a round cutter or a glass to cut circles from the rolled-out dough. The circles should be about 12-15 cm in diameter.
13. Place a spoonful of the cooled filling onto one half of each dough circle, leaving a small border around the edges.
14. Fold the other half of the dough circle over the filling and press the edges together to seal. You can use a fork to crimp the edges for a decorative touch.
15. Place the Jamaican beef patties in zone 1 of the air fryer, ensuring they are not overcrowded.
16. Air fry the patties at 180°C for 15-20 minutes, or until they are golden brown and cooked through.
17. Once cooked, remove the beef patties from the air fryer and let them cool for a few minutes before serving.
18. Serve the Jamaican beef patties warm or at room temperature, and enjoy the deliciously spiced and savoury flavours of this classic Jamaican dish.

Greek Lamb Chops

Serves: 4
Prep time: 10 minutes / Cook time: 10 minutes

Ingredients:
- 600g lamb chops
- 2 tbsp olive oil
- 2 cloves garlic, minced
- 1 tbsp fresh lemon juice
- 1 tsp dried oregano
- Salt and black pepper, to taste

Preparation instructions:
1. Preheat the Ninja Dual Zone Air Fryer to 200°C on zone 1 for 5 minutes.
2. In a bowl, combine the olive oil, minced garlic, lemon juice, dried oregano, salt, and black pepper to make a marinade.
3. Place the lamb chops in a shallow dish and pour the marinade over them. Ensure the chops are evenly coated with the marinade. Let them marinate for 10 minutes.
4. Remove the lamb chops from the marinade, allowing any excess marinade to drip off.
5. Place the lamb chops in zone 1 of the air fryer and cook at 200°C for 8-10 minutes, or until they reach your desired level of doneness.
6. Once cooked, remove the lamb chops from the air fryer and let them rest for a few minutes before serving.
7. Serve the Greek lamb chops hot, accompanied by a side of Greek salad, tzatziki sauce, and roasted potatoes. Enjoy the succulent and flavorful taste of these tender lamb chops.

Brazilian Chicken Heart Skewers

Serves: 4
Prep time: 15 minutes / Cook time: 10 minutes

Ingredients:
- 400g chicken hearts
- 2 tbsp olive oil
- 2 cloves garlic, minced
- 1 tsp paprika
- 1 tsp ground cumin
- 1 tsp dried oregano
- Salt and black pepper, to taste
- Lime wedges, for serving

Preparation instructions:
1. Preheat the Ninja Dual Zone Air Fryer to 200°C on zone 1 for 5 minutes.
2. In a bowl, combine the olive oil, minced garlic, paprika, ground cumin, dried oregano, salt, and black pepper to make a marinade.
3. Place the chicken hearts in a shallow dish

and pour the marinade over them. Ensure the hearts are evenly coated with the marinade. Let them marinate for 15 minutes.
4. Remove the chicken hearts from the marinade, allowing any excess marinade to drip off.
5. Thread the chicken hearts onto skewers, dividing them evenly.
6. Place the skewers in zone 1 of the air fryer and cook at 200°C for 8-10 minutes, or until the chicken hearts are cooked through and nicely charred.
7. Once cooked, remove the skewers from the air fryer and squeeze fresh lime juice over them.
8. Serve the Brazilian chicken heart skewers hot, accompanied by farofa (toasted cassava flour mixture), rice, and vinaigrette sauce. Enjoy the unique and delicious flavours of this Brazilian delicacy.

Jamaican Curry Goat

Serves: 4
Prep time: 20 minutes / Cook time: 1 hour 30 minutes

Ingredients:
- 800g goat meat, cut into bite-sized pieces
- 2 tbsp vegetable oil
- 1 onion, finely chopped
- 3 cloves garlic, minced
- 2 tsp Jamaican curry powder
- 1 tsp ground allspice
- 1 tsp dried thyme
- 1 scotch bonnet pepper, seeded and minced (optional)
- 2 potatoes, peeled and diced
- 2 carrots, peeled and sliced
- 400ml coconut milk
- 400ml chicken or vegetable broth
- Salt and black pepper, to taste
- Fresh cilantro, chopped (for garnish)

Preparation instructions:
1. Preheat the Ninja Dual Zone Air Fryer to 180°C on zone 1 for 5 minutes.
2. In a large pan, heat the vegetable oil over medium heat. Add the chopped onion and minced garlic, and sauté until they are softened and fragrant.
3. Add the goat meat to the pan and brown it on all sides.
4. Sprinkle the Jamaican curry powder, ground allspice, dried thyme, and minced scotch bonnet pepper (if using) over the meat. Stir well to coat the meat with the spices.
5. Add the diced potatoes and sliced carrots to the pan, and pour in the coconut milk and chicken or vegetable broth.
6. Season with salt and black pepper to taste. Bring the mixture to a boil, then reduce the heat to low and simmer for 1 hour 30 minutes, or until the goat meat is tender and the flavours have melded together.
7. Once the curry goat is cooked, remove it from the heat and let it cool slightly.
8. Place the curry goat in a baking dish and place the dish in zone 1 of the air fryer. Cook at 180°C for 10 minutes to further enhance the flavours and thicken the sauce.
9. Once cooked, remove the curry goat from the air fryer and garnish with freshly chopped cilantro.
10. Serve the Jamaican curry goat hot, accompanied by rice and peas, fried plantains, and a side of Jamaican-style coleslaw. Enjoy the rich and aromatic taste of this traditional Jamaican dish.

Korean BBQ Beef Short Ribs

Serves: 4
Prep time: 20 minutes / Cook time: 10 minutes

Ingredients:
- 800g beef short ribs

- 4 tbsp soy sauce
- 2 tbsp brown sugar
- 2 tbsp sesame oil
- 2 cloves garlic, minced
- 1 tbsp grated ginger
- 1 tbsp rice vinegar
- 1 tsp toasted sesame seeds
- 2 green onions, chopped
- Salt and black pepper, to taste

Preparation instructions:

1. Preheat the Ninja Dual Zone Air Fryer to 200°C on zone 1 for 5 minutes.
2. In a bowl, combine the soy sauce, brown sugar, sesame oil, minced garlic, grated ginger, rice vinegar, toasted sesame seeds, chopped green onions, salt, and black pepper to make a marinade.
3. Place the beef short ribs in a shallow dish and pour the marinade over them. Ensure the ribs are evenly coated with the marinade. Let them marinate for 20 minutes.
4. Remove the beef short ribs from the marinade, allowing any excess marinade to drip off.
5. Place the ribs in zone 1 of the air fryer and cook at 200°C for 8-10 minutes, or until they are cooked to your desired level of doneness.
6. Once cooked, remove the beef short ribs from the air fryer and let them rest for a few minutes.
7. Serve the Korean BBQ beef short ribs hot, accompanied by steamed rice, kimchi, and a side of fresh lettuce leaves for wrapping. Enjoy the bold and savoury flavours of this popular Korean dish.

Chinese Five Spice Pork Tenderloin

Serves: 4
Prep time: 10 minutes / Cook time: 15 minutes

Ingredients:
- 600g pork tenderloin
- 2 tbsp soy sauce
- 2 tbsp hoisin sauce
- 1 tbsp honey
- 1 tsp Chinese five spice powder
- 1 tsp grated ginger
- 2 cloves garlic, minced
- 1 tbsp vegetable oil
- Salt and black pepper, to taste
- Fresh cilantro, chopped (for garnish)

Preparation instructions:

1. Preheat the Ninja Dual Zone Air Fryer to 200°C on zone 1 for 5 minutes.
2. In a bowl, whisk together the soy sauce, hoisin sauce, honey, Chinese five spice powder, grated ginger, minced garlic, vegetable oil, salt, and black pepper to make a marinade.
3. Place the pork tenderloin in a shallow dish and pour the marinade over it. Ensure the tenderloin is evenly coated with the marinade. Let it marinate for 10 minutes.
4. Remove the pork tenderloin from the marinade, allowing any excess marinade to drip off.
5. Place the tenderloin in zone 1 of the air fryer and cook at 200°C for 15 minutes, or until the internal temperature reaches 63°C.
6. Once cooked, remove the pork tenderloin from the air fryer and let it rest for a few minutes.
7. Slice the pork tenderloin into medallions and garnish with freshly chopped cilantro.
8. Serve the Chinese five spice pork tenderloin hot, accompanied by steamed rice, stir-fried vegetables, and a drizzle of the reserved

marinade. Enjoy the aromatic and flavorful taste of this Chinese-inspired dish.

Chicken Fried Steak

Serves: 4
Prep time: 15 minutes / Cook time: 15 minutes

Ingredients:
- 4 beef cube steaks (about 150g each)
- 120g all-purpose flour
- 2 tsp paprika
- 1 tsp garlic powder
- 1 tsp onion powder
- 1/2 tsp cayenne pepper
- Salt and black pepper, to taste
- 2 large eggs
- 60ml buttermilk
- Vegetable oil, for frying

Preparation instructions:
1. Preheat the Ninja Dual Zone Air Fryer to 200°C on zone 1 for 5 minutes.
2. In a shallow dish, combine the all-purpose flour, paprika, garlic powder, onion powder, cayenne pepper, salt, and black pepper.
3. In a separate bowl, whisk together the eggs and buttermilk.
4. Dredge each beef cube steak in the flour mixture, coating it thoroughly. Shake off any excess flour.
5. Dip the coated steak into the egg and buttermilk mixture, allowing any excess to drip off.
6. Return the steak to the flour mixture and coat it again, pressing the flour mixture onto the steak to ensure a good coating.
7. Place the coated steaks in zone 1 of the air fryer and drizzle them with vegetable oil.
8. Cook the steaks at 200°C for 15 minutes, flipping them halfway through the cooking time, or until they are golden brown and cooked through.
9. Once cooked, remove the chicken fried steaks from the air fryer and let them rest on a wire rack for a few minutes to allow the coating to crisp up.
10. Serve the chicken fried steaks hot, accompanied by mashed potatoes, country gravy, and a side of steamed vegetables. Enjoy the crispy and flavorful goodness of this classic Southern dish.

Chicken Parmesan

Serves: 4
Prep time: 20 minutes / Cook time: 15 minutes

Ingredients:
- 4 boneless, skinless chicken breasts
- 120g breadcrumbs
- 50g grated Parmesan cheese
- 1 tsp dried oregano
- 1/2 tsp garlic powder
- Salt and black pepper, to taste
- 2 large eggs, beaten
- 60ml milk
- 250g marinara sauce
- 150g shredded mozzarella cheese
- Fresh basil leaves, for garnish

Preparation instructions:
1. Preheat the Ninja Dual Zone Air Fryer to 200°C on zone 1 for 5 minutes.
2. In a shallow dish, combine the breadcrumbs, grated Parmesan cheese, dried oregano, garlic powder, salt, and black pepper.
3. In a separate bowl, whisk together the beaten eggs and milk.
4. Dredge each chicken breast in the breadcrumb mixture, coating it thoroughly. Press the breadcrumbs onto the chicken to ensure a good coating.
5. Dip the coated chicken into the egg and milk mixture, allowing any excess to drip off.
6. Return the chicken to the breadcrumb mixture and coat it again, pressing the

breadcrumbs onto the chicken to create a thick crust.
7. Place the coated chicken breasts in zone 1 of the air fryer and cook at 200°C for 15 minutes, or until they are cooked through and the crust is golden brown.
8. Once cooked, remove the chicken breasts from the air fryer and spoon marinara sauce over each breast.
9. Sprinkle the shredded mozzarella cheese on top of the sauce.
10. Return the chicken to the air fryer and cook for an additional 2-3 minutes, or until the cheese is melted and bubbly.
11. Once melted, remove the chicken Parmesan from the air fryer and garnish with fresh basil leaves.
12. Serve the chicken Parmesan hot, accompanied by spaghetti or your favourite pasta, and additional marinara sauce. Enjoy the delicious combination of crispy chicken, tangy sauce, and melted cheese in this classic Italian dish.

Breaded Veal Cutlets

Serves: 4
Prep time: 15 minutes / Cook time: 12 minutes

Ingredients:
- 4 veal cutlets (about 150g each)
- 120g breadcrumbs
- 50g grated Parmesan cheese
- 1 tsp dried parsley
- 1/2 tsp garlic powder
- Salt and black pepper, to taste
- 2 large eggs, beaten
- 60ml milk
- Vegetable oil, for frying

Preparation instructions:
1. Preheat the Ninja Dual Zone Air Fryer to 200°C on zone 1 for 5 minutes.
2. In a shallow dish, combine the breadcrumbs, grated Parmesan cheese, dried parsley, garlic powder, salt, and black pepper.
3. In a separate bowl, whisk together the beaten eggs and milk.
4. Dredge each veal cutlet in the breadcrumb mixture, coating it thoroughly. Press the breadcrumbs onto the cutlet to ensure a good coating.
5. Dip the coated cutlet into the egg and milk mixture, allowing any excess to drip off.
6. Return the cutlet to the breadcrumb mixture and coat it again, pressing the breadcrumbs onto the cutlet to create a thick crust.
7. Place the coated veal cutlets in zone 1 of the air fryer and drizzle them with vegetable oil.
8. Cook the cutlets at 200°C for 12 minutes, flipping them halfway through the cooking time, or until they are golden brown and cooked through.
9. Once cooked, remove the breaded veal cutlets from the air fryer and let them rest on a wire rack for a few minutes to allow the coating to crisp up.
10. Serve the breaded veal cutlets hot, accompanied by lemon wedges, a side of mashed potatoes or pasta, and a fresh green salad. Enjoy the tender and flavorful veal in this classic breaded dish.

Southern Fried Chicken

Serves: 4
Prep time: 20 minutes / Cook time: 20 minutes

Ingredients:
- 8 chicken drumsticks
- 120g all-purpose flour
- 2 tsp paprika
- 1 tsp garlic powder
- 1 tsp onion powder
- 1/2 tsp cayenne pepper
- Salt and black pepper, to taste
- 2 large eggs

- 60ml buttermilk
- Vegetable oil, for frying

Preparation instructions:
1. Preheat the Ninja Dual Zone Air Fryer to 200°C on zone 1 for 5 minutes.
2. In a shallow dish, combine the all-purpose flour, paprika, garlic powder, onion powder, cayenne pepper, salt, and black pepper.
3. In a separate bowl, whisk together the eggs and buttermilk.
4. Dredge each chicken drumstick in the flour mixture, coating it thoroughly. Shake off any excess flour.
5. Dip the coated drumstick into the egg and buttermilk mixture, allowing any excess to drip off.
6. Return the drumstick to the flour mixture and coat it again, pressing the flour mixture onto the chicken to ensure a good coating.
7. Place the coated drumsticks in zone 1 of the air fryer and drizzle them with vegetable oil.
8. Cook the drumsticks at 200°C for 20 minutes, flipping them halfway through the cooking time, or until they are golden brown and cooked through.
9. Once cooked, remove the southern fried chicken from the air fryer and let them rest on a wire rack for a few minutes to allow the coating to crisp up.
10. Serve the southern fried chicken hot, accompanied by mashed potatoes, coleslaw, and a side of biscuits. Enjoy the crispy and flavorful taste of this classic Southern favourite.

Crispy Pork Schnitzel

Serves: 4
Prep time: 15 minutes / Cook time: 12 minutes

Ingredients:
- 4 pork schnitzels (about 150g each)
- 120g breadcrumbs
- 50g grated Parmesan cheese
- 1 tsp dried parsley
- 1/2 tsp garlic powder
- Salt and black pepper, to taste
- 2 large eggs, beaten
- 60ml milk
- Vegetable oil, for frying

Preparation instructions:
1. Preheat the Ninja Dual Zone Air Fryer to 200°C on zone 1 for 5 minutes.
2. In a shallow dish, combine the breadcrumbs, grated Parmesan cheese, dried parsley, garlic powder, salt, and black pepper.
3. In a separate bowl, whisk together the beaten eggs and milk.
4. Dredge each pork schnitzel in the breadcrumb mixture, coating it thoroughly. Press the breadcrumbs onto the schnitzel to ensure a good coating.
5. Dip the coated schnitzel into the egg and milk mixture, allowing any excess to drip off.
6. Return the schnitzel to the breadcrumb mixture and coat it again, pressing the breadcrumbs onto the schnitzel to create a thick crust.
7. Place the coated pork schnitzels in zone 1 of the air fryer and drizzle them with vegetable oil.
8. Cook the schnitzels at 200°C for 12 minutes, flipping them halfway through the cooking time, or until they are golden brown and cooked through.
9. Once cooked, remove the crispy pork schnitzels from the air fryer and let them rest on a wire rack for a few minutes to allow the coating to crisp up.
10. Serve the crispy pork schnitzels hot, accompanied by lemon wedges, mashed potatoes, and a side of sautéed vegetables. Enjoy the delicious and crispy goodness of

this traditional German dish.

Chicken Nuggets

Serves: 4
Prep time: 15 minutes / Cook time: 12 minutes

Ingredients:
- 500g boneless, skinless chicken breasts, cut into bite-sized pieces
- 120g breadcrumbs
- 50g grated Parmesan cheese
- 1 tsp dried parsley
- 1/2 tsp garlic powder
- Salt and black pepper, to taste
- 2 large eggs, beaten
- 60ml milk
- Vegetable oil, for frying

Preparation instructions:
1. Preheat the Ninja Dual Zone Air Fryer to 200°C on zone 1 for 5 minutes.
2. In a shallow dish, combine the breadcrumbs, grated Parmesan cheese, dried parsley, garlic powder, salt, and black pepper.
3. In a separate bowl, whisk together the beaten eggs and milk.
4. Dredge each chicken piece in the breadcrumb mixture, coating it thoroughly. Press the breadcrumbs onto the chicken to ensure a good coating.
5. Dip the coated chicken into the egg and milk mixture, allowing any excess to drip off.
6. Return the chicken to the breadcrumb mixture and coat it again, pressing the breadcrumbs onto the chicken to create a thick crust.
7. Place the coated chicken nuggets in zone 1 of the air fryer and drizzle them with vegetable oil.
8. Cook the nuggets at 200°C for 12 minutes, flipping them halfway through the cooking time, or until they are golden brown and cooked through.
9. Once cooked, remove the chicken nuggets from the air fryer and let them rest on a wire rack for a few minutes to allow the coating to crisp up.
10. Serve the chicken nuggets hot, accompanied by your favourite dipping sauces and a side of French fries or sweet potato fries. Enjoy these crispy and flavorful bite-sized treats!

Chapter 5: Healthy Vegetables and Sides

Cauliflower "Steak"

Serves: 4
Prep time: 10 minutes / Cook time: 20 minutes

Ingredients:
- 1 large cauliflower head, sliced into thick "steaks"
- 2 tbsp olive oil
- 2 cloves garlic, minced
- 1 tsp smoked paprika
- 1/2 tsp dried thyme
- Salt and black pepper, to taste

Preparation instructions:
1. Preheat the Ninja Dual Zone Air Fryer to 200°C on zone 1 for 5 minutes.
2. In a small bowl, mix together the olive oil, minced garlic, smoked paprika, dried thyme, salt, and black pepper.
3. Brush both sides of the cauliflower "steaks" with the seasoned oil mixture.
4. Place the cauliflower "steaks" in zone 1 of the air fryer.
5. Cook the cauliflower at 200°C for 20 minutes, flipping them halfway through the cooking time, or until they are tender and lightly browned.
6. Once cooked, remove the cauliflower "steaks" from the air fryer and let them cool for a few minutes before serving.
7. Serve the cauliflower "steaks" as a main dish or as a side to accompany your favourite meals. Enjoy the delicious and nutritious alternative to traditional steak!

Broccoli and Carrots

Serves: 4
Prep time: 10 minutes / Cook time: 12 minutes

Ingredients:
- 300g broccoli florets
- 200g carrots, sliced into sticks
- 2 tbsp olive oil
- 2 cloves garlic, minced
- Salt and black pepper, to taste

Preparation instructions:
1. Preheat the Ninja Dual Zone Air Fryer to 200°C on zone 1 for 5 minutes.
2. In a bowl, combine the broccoli florets, carrot sticks, olive oil, minced garlic, salt, and black pepper. Toss until the vegetables are evenly coated.
3. Place the seasoned vegetables in zone 1 of the air fryer.
4. Cook the broccoli and carrots at 200°C for 12 minutes, shaking the basket halfway through the cooking time, or until they are tender-crisp and lightly browned.
5. Once cooked, remove the broccoli and carrots from the air fryer and let them cool for a few minutes before serving.
6. Serve the broccoli and carrots as a delicious and nutritious side dish to complement your main course. Enjoy the vibrant flavours and crisp texture!

Green Beans with Garlic

Serves: 4
Prep time: 10 minutes / Cook time: 12 minutes

Ingredients:
- 300g green beans, trimmed
- 2 tbsp olive oil
- 2 cloves garlic, minced
- Salt and black pepper, to taste

Preparation instructions:
1. Preheat the Ninja Dual Zone Air Fryer to 200°C on zone 1 for 5 minutes.
2. In a bowl, combine the green beans, olive oil, minced garlic, salt, and black pepper.

Toss until the green beans are evenly coated.
3. Place the seasoned green beans in zone 1 of the air fryer.
4. Cook the green beans at 200°C for 12 minutes, shaking the basket halfway through the cooking time, or until they are tender-crisp and lightly browned.
5. Once cooked, remove the green beans from the air fryer and let them cool for a few minutes before serving.
6. Serve the green beans as a healthy and flavorful side dish. Enjoy the vibrant green colour and the aromatic garlic-infused taste!

Roasted Garlic Mushrooms

Serves: 4
Prep time: 10 minutes / Cook time: 12 minutes

Ingredients:
- 400g button mushrooms, cleaned and halved
- 2 tbsp olive oil
- 3 cloves garlic, minced
- 1 tbsp chopped fresh parsley
- Salt and black pepper, to taste

Preparation instructions:
1. Preheat the Ninja Dual Zone Air Fryer to 200°C on zone 1 for 5 minutes.
2. In a bowl, combine the mushrooms, olive oil, minced garlic, chopped parsley, salt, and black pepper. Toss until the mushrooms are evenly coated.
3. Place the seasoned mushrooms in zone 1 of the air fryer.
4. Cook the mushrooms at 200°C for 12 minutes, shaking the basket halfway through the cooking time, or until they are tender and golden brown.
5. Once cooked, remove the mushrooms from the air fryer and let them cool for a few minutes before serving.
6. Serve the roasted garlic mushrooms as a flavorful side dish or as a topping for salads, pasta, or grilled meats. Enjoy the rich and earthy flavours!

Eggplant Fries

Serves: 4
Prep time: 15 minutes / Cook time: 15 minutes

Ingredients:
- 1 large eggplant
- 60g all-purpose flour
- 2 large eggs, beaten
- 120g breadcrumbs
- 1 tsp dried oregano
- 1/2 tsp garlic powder
- Salt and black pepper, to taste
- Olive oil spray

Preparation instructions:
1. Preheat the Ninja Dual Zone Air Fryer to 200°C on zone 1 for 5 minutes.
2. Cut the eggplant into fry-shaped sticks.
3. Place the flour in a shallow dish. In another dish, beat the eggs. In a third dish, combine the breadcrumbs, dried oregano, garlic powder, salt, and black pepper.
4. Dip each eggplant stick into the flour, then into the beaten eggs, and finally coat it with the breadcrumb mixture. Press the breadcrumbs onto the eggplant to ensure a good coating.
5. Place the coated eggplant fries in zone 1 of the air fryer. Spray them with olive oil spray to promote browning.
6. Cook the eggplant fries at 200°C for 15 minutes, flipping them halfway through the cooking time, or until they are crispy and golden brown.
7. Once cooked, remove the eggplant fries from the air fryer and let them cool for a few minutes before serving.
8. Serve the eggplant fries as a delicious and healthier alternative to traditional fries. Enjoy the crispy texture and the delicate flavour of the eggplant!

Spicy Okra

Serves: 4
Prep time: 10 minutes / Cook time: 12 minutes

Ingredients:
- 300g okra, trimmed and halved lengthwise
- 2 tbsp olive oil
- 1/2 tsp ground cumin
- 1/2 tsp paprika
- 1/4 tsp cayenne pepper (adjust to taste)
- Salt and black pepper, to taste

Preparation instructions:
1. Preheat the Ninja Dual Zone Air Fryer to 200°C on zone 1 for 5 minutes.
2. In a bowl, combine the okra, olive oil, ground cumin, paprika, cayenne pepper, salt, and black pepper. Toss until the okra is evenly coated with the spice mixture.
3. Place the seasoned okra in zone 1 of the air fryer.
4. Cook the okra at 200°C for 12 minutes, shaking the basket halfway through the cooking time, or until the okra is tender-crisp and lightly browned.
5. Once cooked, remove the okra from the air fryer and let it cool for a few minutes before serving.
6. Serve the spicy okra as a tasty side dish or as a snack. Enjoy the combination of flavours and the satisfying crunch of the okra!

Butternut Squash Wedges

Serves: 4
Prep time: 10 minutes / Cook time: 20 minutes

Ingredients:
- 600g butternut squash, peeled and cut into wedges
- 2 tbsp olive oil
- 1 tsp smoked paprika
- 1/2 tsp ground cumin
- Salt and black pepper, to taste

Preparation instructions:
1. Preheat the Ninja Dual Zone Air Fryer to 200°C on zone 1 for 5 minutes.
2. In a bowl, toss the butternut squash wedges with olive oil, smoked paprika, ground cumin, salt, and black pepper until well coated.
3. Place the seasoned butternut squash wedges in zone 1 of the air fryer.
4. Cook the wedges at 200°C for 20 minutes, shaking the basket halfway through the cooking time, or until they are tender and lightly browned.
5. Once cooked, remove the butternut squash wedges from the air fryer and let them cool for a few minutes before serving.
6. Serve the butternut squash wedges as a delicious and nutritious side dish. Enjoy the sweet and savoury flavours!

Roasted Carrot Fries

Serves: 4
Prep time: 10 minutes / Cook time: 18 minutes

Ingredients:
- 500g carrots, peeled and cut into fries
- 2 tbsp olive oil
- 1 tsp ground cumin
- 1/2 tsp paprika
- Salt and black pepper, to taste

Preparation instructions:
1. Preheat the Ninja Dual Zone Air Fryer to 200°C on zone 1 for 5 minutes.
2. In a bowl, toss the carrot fries with olive oil, ground cumin, paprika, salt, and black pepper until well coated.
3. Place the seasoned carrot fries in zone 1 of the air fryer.
4. Cook the fries at 200°C for 18 minutes, shaking the basket halfway through the cooking time, or until they are crispy and golden brown.
5. Once cooked, remove the carrot fries from the air fryer and let them cool for a few

minutes before serving.
6. Serve the roasted carrot fries as a healthy and flavorful alternative to traditional fries. Enjoy the natural sweetness and the satisfying crunch!

Garlic Parmesan Broccoli

Serves: 4
Prep time: 10 minutes / Cook time: 10 minutes

Ingredients:
- 500g broccoli florets
- 2 tbsp olive oil
- 3 cloves garlic, minced
- 2 tbsp grated Parmesan cheese
- Salt and black pepper, to taste

Preparation instructions:
1. Preheat the Ninja Dual Zone Air Fryer to 200°C on zone 1 for 5 minutes.
2. In a bowl, toss the broccoli florets with olive oil, minced garlic, grated Parmesan cheese, salt, and black pepper until well coated.
3. Place the seasoned broccoli florets in zone 1 of the air fryer.
4. Cook the broccoli at 200°C for 10 minutes, shaking the basket halfway through the cooking time, or until they are tender and slightly charred.
5. Once cooked, remove the garlic Parmesan broccoli from the air fryer and let it cool for a few minutes before serving.
6. Serve the flavorful garlic Parmesan broccoli as a nutritious side dish. Enjoy the combination of garlicky, cheesy, and roasted flavours!

Cinnamon Roasted Sweet Potatoes

Serves: 4
Prep time: 10 minutes / Cook time: 18 minutes

Ingredients:
- 600g sweet potatoes, peeled and cut into cubes
- 2 tbsp olive oil
- 1 tsp ground cinnamon
- 1/2 tsp ground nutmeg
- Salt, to taste

Preparation instructions:
1. Preheat the Ninja Dual Zone Air Fryer to 200°C on zone 1 for 5 minutes.
2. In a bowl, toss the sweet potato cubes with olive oil, ground cinnamon, ground nutmeg, and salt until well coated.
3. Place the seasoned sweet potatoes in zone 1 of the air fryer.
4. Cook the sweet potatoes at 200°C for 18 minutes, shaking the basket halfway through the cooking time, or until they are tender and caramelised.
5. Once cooked, remove the cinnamon roasted sweet potatoes from the air fryer and let them cool for a few minutes before serving.
6. Serve the sweet and fragrant cinnamon roasted sweet potatoes as a delightful side dish. Enjoy the comforting flavours of cinnamon and nutmeg!

Sautéed Spinach with Garlic

Serves: 4
Prep time: 5 minutes / Cook time: 5 minutes

Ingredients:
- 300g fresh spinach leaves
- 2 cloves garlic, minced
- 1 tbsp olive oil
- Salt and black pepper, to taste

Preparation instructions:
1. Preheat the Ninja Dual Zone Air Fryer to 180°C on zone 1 for 5 minutes.
2. Heat the olive oil in a pan over medium heat.
3. Add the minced garlic to the pan and sauté for about 1 minute until fragrant.
4. Add the fresh spinach leaves to the pan and sauté for 2-3 minutes until wilted.

5. Season with salt and black pepper, adjusting the amount to taste.
6. Once cooked, remove the sautéed spinach from the pan and let it cool for a few minutes before serving.
7. Serve the flavorful sautéed spinach as a nutritious side dish. Enjoy the vibrant green colour and the aromatic garlic!

Grilled Portobello Mushrooms

Serves: 4
Prep time: 10 minutes / Cook time: 10 minutes

Ingredients:
- 4 large Portobello mushrooms
- 2 tbsp balsamic vinegar
- 2 tbsp olive oil
- 2 cloves garlic, minced
- Salt and black pepper, to taste

Preparation instructions:
1. Preheat the Ninja Dual Zone Air Fryer to 200°C on zone 1 for 5 minutes.
2. In a bowl, whisk together the balsamic vinegar, olive oil, minced garlic, salt, and black pepper.
3. Place the Portobello mushrooms in a shallow dish and pour the marinade over them, ensuring all sides are coated.
4. Let the mushrooms marinate for 5 minutes.
5. Place the marinated mushrooms in zone 1 of the air fryer.
6. Cook the mushrooms at 200°C for 10 minutes, flipping them halfway through the cooking time, or until they are tender and slightly charred.
7. Once cooked, remove the grilled Portobello mushrooms from the air fryer and let them cool for a few minutes before serving.
8. Serve the flavorful grilled Portobello mushrooms as a delicious vegetarian option. Enjoy the meaty texture and the tangy balsamic flavour!

Roasted Balsamic Brussel Sprouts

Serves: 4
Prep time: 10 minutes / Cook time: 15 minutes

Ingredients:
- 500g Brussels sprouts, halved
- 2 tbsp balsamic vinegar
- 2 tbsp olive oil
- 1 tbsp honey (optional, for sweetness)
- Salt and black pepper, to taste

Preparation instructions:
1. Preheat the Ninja Dual Zone Air Fryer to 200°C on zone 1 for 5 minutes.
2. In a bowl, whisk together the balsamic vinegar, olive oil, honey (if using), salt, and black pepper.
3. Place the halved Brussels sprouts in a shallow dish and pour the marinade over them, ensuring all sides are coated.
4. Let the Brussels sprouts marinate for 5 minutes.
5. Place the marinated Brussels sprouts in zone 1 of the air fryer.
6. Cook the Brussels sprouts at 200°C for 15 minutes, shaking the basket halfway through the cooking time, or until they are tender and caramelised.
7. Once cooked, remove the roasted balsamic Brussels sprouts from the air fryer and let them cool for a few minutes before serving.
8. Serve the tangy and sweet roasted balsamic Brussels sprouts as a delightful side dish. Enjoy the crispy outer leaves and the tender centres!

Sesame Soy Broccoli

Serves: 4
Prep time: 10 minutes / Cook time: 8 minutes

Ingredients:
- 500g broccoli florets

- 2 tbsp soy sauce
- 1 tbsp sesame oil
- 1 tbsp sesame seeds
- 2 cloves garlic, minced
- Salt and black pepper, to taste

Preparation instructions:

1. Preheat the Ninja Dual Zone Air Fryer to 200°C on zone 1 for 5 minutes.
2. In a bowl, whisk together the soy sauce, sesame oil, sesame seeds, minced garlic, salt, and black pepper.
3. Place the broccoli florets in a shallow dish and pour the marinade over them, ensuring all sides are coated.
4. Let the broccoli florets marinate for 5 minutes.
5. Place the marinated broccoli florets in zone 1 of the air fryer.
6. Cook the broccoli at 200°C for 8 minutes, shaking the basket halfway through the cooking time, or until they are tender-crisp and lightly charred.
7. Once cooked, remove the sesame soy broccoli from the air fryer and let it cool for a few minutes before serving.
8. Serve the flavorful sesame soy broccoli as a tasty and healthy side dish. Enjoy the nutty sesame and savoury soy flavours!

Roasted Garlic and Rosemary Potatoes

Serves: 4
Prep time: 10 minutes / Cook time: 25 minutes

Ingredients:

- 600g baby potatoes, halved
- 3 cloves garlic, minced
- 2 tbsp olive oil
- 1 tbsp chopped fresh rosemary
- Salt and black pepper, to taste

Preparation instructions:

1. Preheat the Ninja Dual Zone Air Fryer to 200°C on zone 1 for 5 minutes.
2. In a bowl, toss the halved baby potatoes with minced garlic, olive oil, chopped fresh rosemary, salt, and black pepper until well coated.
3. Place the seasoned potatoes in zone 1 of the air fryer.
4. Cook the potatoes at 200°C for 25 minutes, shaking the basket halfway through the cooking time, or until they are golden brown and crispy on the outside and tender on the inside.
5. Once cooked, remove the roasted garlic and rosemary potatoes from the air fryer and let them cool for a few minutes before serving.
6. Serve the aromatic and flavorful roasted garlic and rosemary potatoes as a delightful side dish. Enjoy the crispy exteriors and the soft centres!

Lemon Herb Roasted Cauliflower

Serves: 4
Prep time: 10 minutes / Cook time: 20 minutes

Ingredients:

- 1 large head of cauliflower, cut into florets
- 2 tbsp olive oil
- Zest of 1 lemon
- Juice of 1 lemon
- 1 tbsp chopped fresh parsley
- 1 tsp dried thyme
- Salt and black pepper, to taste

Preparation instructions:

1. Preheat the Ninja Dual Zone Air Fryer to 200°C on zone 1 for 5 minutes.
2. In a bowl, toss the cauliflower florets with olive oil, lemon zest, lemon juice, chopped fresh parsley, dried thyme, salt, and black pepper until well coated.
3. Place the seasoned cauliflower florets in zone 1 of the air fryer.
4. Cook the cauliflower at 200°C for 20

minutes, shaking the basket halfway through the cooking time, or until they are tender and lightly browned.
5. Once cooked, remove the lemon herb roasted cauliflower from the air fryer and let it cool for a few minutes before serving.
6. Serve the zesty and fragrant lemon herb roasted cauliflower as a flavorful side dish. Enjoy the tangy lemon and aromatic herbs!

Parmesan Roasted Acorn Squash

Serves: 4
Prep time: 10 minutes / Cook time: 25 minutes

Ingredients:
- 2 acorn squash, halved and seeds removed
- 2 tbsp olive oil
- 60g grated Parmesan cheese
- 1 tsp dried thyme
- Salt and black pepper, to taste

Preparation instructions:
1. Preheat the Ninja Dual Zone Air Fryer to 200°C on zone 1 for 5 minutes.
2. Brush the cut sides of the acorn squash halves with olive oil.
3. In a small bowl, mix together the grated Parmesan cheese, dried thyme, salt, and black pepper.
4. Sprinkle the Parmesan cheese mixture evenly over the cut sides of the acorn squash halves.
5. Place the seasoned acorn squash halves in zone 1 of the air fryer, cut side up.
6. Cook the acorn squash at 200°C for 25 minutes or until they are tender and the cheese is golden and slightly crispy.
7. Once cooked, remove the Parmesan roasted acorn squash from the air fryer and let it cool for a few minutes before serving.
8. Serve the savoury and cheesy Parmesan roasted acorn squash as a delightful side dish. Enjoy the combination of flavours and textures!

Curried Cauliflower Rice

Serves: 4
Prep time: 10 minutes / Cook time: 10 minutes

Ingredients:
- 1 head of cauliflower, florets only
- 2 tbsp olive oil
- 1 onion, finely chopped
- 2 cloves garlic, minced
- 1 tbsp curry powder
- 1/2 tsp ground cumin
- 1/2 tsp ground coriander
- Salt and black pepper, to taste
- Fresh cilantro, for garnish (optional)

Preparation instructions:
1. Preheat the Ninja Dual Zone Air Fryer to 180°C on zone 1 for 5 minutes.
2. Place the cauliflower florets in a food processor and pulse until they resemble rice-like grains.
3. Heat the olive oil in a pan or skillet over medium heat.
4. Add the chopped onion and minced garlic to the pan and sauté for about 2 minutes until softened.
5. Add the cauliflower rice to the pan and cook for 5-6 minutes, stirring occasionally, until it is tender.
6. Sprinkle the curry powder, ground cumin, ground coriander, salt, and black pepper over the cauliflower rice. Stir well to combine and cook for another 2 minutes to allow the flavours to meld.
7. Once cooked, remove the curried cauliflower rice from the pan and let it cool for a few minutes before serving.
8. Garnish with fresh cilantro, if desired, and serve the flavorful curried cauliflower rice as a delicious and healthy side dish. Enjoy the aromatic spices and the tender texture!

Chapter 6: Fast and Easy Everyday Favourites

Grilled Cheese

Serves: 2
Prep time: 5 minutes / Cook time: 8 minutes

Ingredients:
- 4 slices of bread
- 100g cheddar cheese, grated
- Butter, for spreading

Preparation instructions:
1. Preheat the Ninja Dual Zone Air Fryer to 200°C on zone 1 for 5 minutes.
2. Spread butter on one side of each bread slice.
3. Place half of the grated cheddar cheese on the unbuttered side of 2 bread slices.
4. Top the cheese with the remaining 2 bread slices, buttered side up.
5. Place the sandwiches in zone 1 of the air fryer.
6. Cook the sandwiches at 200°C for 4 minutes, then flip them over.
7. Cook for an additional 4 minutes or until the cheese is melted and the bread is golden and crispy.
8. Once cooked, remove the grilled cheese sandwiches from the air fryer and let them cool for a minute before serving.
9. Cut the sandwiches in half and enjoy the gooey and comforting grilled cheese!

Bacon Wrapped Shrimp

Serves: 4
Prep time: 15 minutes / Cook time: 10 minutes

Ingredients:
- 16 large shrimp, peeled and deveined
- 8 slices of bacon, cut in half lengthwise
- Salt and black pepper, to taste
- Wooden toothpicks, soaked in water for 15 minutes

Preparation instructions:
1. Preheat the Ninja Dual Zone Air Fryer to 200°C on zone 1 for 5 minutes.
2. Season the shrimp with salt and black pepper.
3. Wrap each shrimp with a half slice of bacon and secure with a toothpick.
4. Place the bacon-wrapped shrimp in zone 1 of the air fryer.
5. Cook the shrimp at 200°C for 8-10 minutes, turning halfway through, or until the bacon is crispy and the shrimp are cooked through.
6. Once cooked, remove the bacon-wrapped shrimp from the air fryer and let them cool for a few minutes before serving.
7. Serve the succulent and savoury bacon-wrapped shrimp as a delightful appetiser or main dish.

Mozzarella Sticks

Serves: 4
Prep time: 15 minutes / Cook time: 8 minutes

Ingredients:
- 200g mozzarella cheese, cut into sticks
- 80g breadcrumbs
- 40g grated Parmesan cheese
- 1 tsp dried oregano
- 1 tsp dried basil
- 2 large eggs, beaten
- Marinara sauce, for dipping

Preparation instructions:
1. Preheat the Ninja Dual Zone Air Fryer to 200°C on zone 1 for 5 minutes.
2. In a shallow bowl, combine the breadcrumbs, grated Parmesan cheese, dried oregano, and dried basil.
3. Dip each mozzarella stick into the beaten eggs, then roll it in the breadcrumb mixture, pressing gently to adhere.

4. Place the coated mozzarella sticks in zone 1 of the air fryer.
5. Cook the mozzarella sticks at 200°C for 6-8 minutes, or until the cheese is melted and the coating is golden and crispy.
6. Once cooked, remove the mozzarella sticks from the air fryer and let them cool for a minute before serving.
7. Serve the mozzarella sticks with marinara sauce for dipping. Enjoy the gooey cheese and crunchy coating!

BBQ Chicken Legs

Serves: 4
Prep time: 10 minutes / Cook time: 25 minutes

Ingredients:
- 8 chicken legs
- 120ml BBQ sauce
- 2 tbsp olive oil
- 1 tsp paprika
- 1/2 tsp garlic powder
- 1/2 tsp onion powder
- Salt and black pepper, to taste

Preparation instructions:
1. Preheat the Ninja Dual Zone Air Fryer to 200°C on zone 1 for 5 minutes.
2. In a bowl, whisk together the BBQ sauce, olive oil, paprika, garlic powder, onion powder, salt, and black pepper.
3. Place the chicken legs in a ziplock bag and pour the BBQ sauce mixture over them. Seal the bag and massage the sauce into the chicken to coat evenly. Let it marinate for 5 minutes.
4. Place the chicken legs in zone 1 of the air fryer, leaving space between them.
5. Cook the chicken legs at 200°C for 20-25 minutes, flipping them halfway through, or until they reach an internal temperature of 75°C and the skin is crispy and caramelised.
6. Once cooked, remove the BBQ chicken legs from the air fryer and let them rest for a few minutes before serving.
7. Serve the delicious and flavorful BBQ chicken legs as a finger-licking main dish.

Garlic Bread

Serves: 4
Prep time: 5 minutes / Cook time: 6 minutes

Ingredients:
- 1 baguette or loaf of bread
- 60g unsalted butter, softened
- 2 cloves of garlic, minced
- 1 tbsp chopped fresh parsley
- Salt, to taste

Preparation instructions:
1. Preheat the Ninja Dual Zone Air Fryer to 200°C on zone 1 for 5 minutes.
2. Cut the baguette or loaf of bread into desired-sized slices.
3. In a small bowl, mix together the softened butter, minced garlic, chopped fresh parsley, and salt.
4. Spread the garlic butter mixture on one side of each bread slice.
5. Place the garlic bread slices in zone 1 of the air fryer.
6. Cook the garlic bread at 200°C for 4-6 minutes, or until the bread is toasted and the butter is melted and infused with garlic flavour.
7. Once cooked, remove the garlic bread from the air fryer and let it cool for a minute before serving.
8. Serve the aromatic and buttery garlic bread as a delectable accompaniment to soups, pasta, or as a snack.

Crispy Fried Chicken

Serves: 4
Prep time: 10 minutes / Cook time: 25 minutes

Ingredients:
- 8 chicken drumsticks
- 100g all-purpose flour
- 1 tsp paprika
- 1/2 tsp garlic powder
- 1/2 tsp onion powder
- 1/2 tsp dried thyme
- Salt and black pepper, to taste
- 2 large eggs, beaten
- Vegetable oil, for frying

Preparation instructions:
1. Preheat the Ninja Dual Zone Air Fryer to 200°C on zone 1 for 5 minutes.
2. In a shallow bowl, mix together the all-purpose flour, paprika, garlic powder, onion powder, dried thyme, salt, and black pepper.
3. Dip each chicken drumstick into the beaten eggs, then coat it in the seasoned flour mixture, pressing gently to adhere.
4. Place the coated chicken drumsticks in zone 1 of the air fryer, leaving space between them.
5. Cook the chicken drumsticks at 200°C for 20-25 minutes, flipping them halfway through, or until the chicken is cooked through and the coating is golden and crispy.
6. Once cooked, remove the crispy fried chicken from the air fryer and let it rest for a few minutes before serving.
7. Serve the irresistibly crunchy and flavorful fried chicken as a satisfying main dish.

Baked Potatoes

Serves: 4
Prep time: 5 minutes / Cook time: 40 minutes

Ingredients:
- 4 medium-sized potatoes
- Olive oil, for brushing
- Salt, to taste
- Toppings of your choice (e.g., sour cream, chives, grated cheese)

Preparation instructions:
1. Preheat the Ninja Dual Zone Air Fryer to 200°C on zone 1 for 5 minutes.
2. Wash and dry the potatoes. Prick each potato several times with a fork.
3. Brush the potatoes with olive oil and sprinkle them with salt.
4. Place the potatoes in zone 1 of the air fryer, leaving space between them.
5. Cook the potatoes at 200°C for 40-45 minutes, or until they are tender and the skins are crispy.
6. Once cooked, remove the baked potatoes from the air fryer and let them cool for a few minutes.
7. Cut a slit in each potato and fluff the insides with a fork.
8. Serve the baked potatoes with your favourite toppings, such as sour cream, chives, or grated cheese, for a comforting and versatile dish.

Grilled Burgers

Serves: 4
Prep time: 10 minutes / Cook time: 12 minutes

Ingredients:
- 500g ground beef
- 1/2 tsp onion powder
- 1/2 tsp garlic powder
- 1/2 tsp paprika
- Salt and black pepper, to taste
- 4 burger buns
- Lettuce, tomato slices, onion slices, and condiments of your choice

Preparation instructions:
1. Preheat the Ninja Dual Zone Air Fryer to 200°C on zone 1 for 5 minutes.
2. In a bowl, combine the ground beef, onion powder, garlic powder, paprika, salt, and black pepper. Mix well.
3. Divide the beef mixture into 4 equal portions

and shape them into burger patties.
4. Place the burger patties in zone 1 of the air fryer.
5. Cook the burgers at 200°C for 6 minutes, then flip them over.
6. Cook for an additional 6 minutes or until the burgers reach your desired level of doneness.
7. Once cooked, remove the grilled burgers from the air fryer and let them rest for a few minutes.
8. Toast the burger buns if desired. Assemble the burgers with lettuce, tomato slices, onion slices, and condiments of your choice.
9. Serve the juicy and flavorful grilled burgers for a satisfying meal.

Nachos

Serves: 4
Prep time: 10 minutes / Cook time: 8 minutes

Ingredients:
- 200g tortilla chips
- 150g grated cheddar cheese
- 150g cooked ground beef or shredded chicken
- 1/2 tsp chilli powder
- 1/2 tsp cumin
- 1/4 tsp garlic powder
- 1/4 tsp onion powder
- Sliced jalapenos, diced tomatoes, sliced black olives, sour cream, and guacamole, for topping

Preparation instructions:
1. Preheat the Ninja Dual Zone Air Fryer to 200°C on zone 1 for 5 minutes.
2. In a bowl, mix together the cooked ground beef or shredded chicken with the chilli powder, cumin, garlic powder, and onion powder.
3. Spread the tortilla chips in a single layer in zone 1 of the air fryer.
4. Sprinkle half of the grated cheddar cheese evenly over the tortilla chips.
5. Spoon the seasoned ground beef or shredded chicken mixture over the cheese.
6. Sprinkle the remaining grated cheddar cheese on top.
7. Add sliced jalapenos, diced tomatoes, and sliced black olives as desired.
8. Cook the nachos at 200°C for 6-8 minutes, or until the cheese is melted and bubbly.
9. Once cooked, remove the nachos from the air fryer and let them cool for a minute.
10. Serve the loaded nachos with sour cream and guacamole for a crowd-pleasing appetiser or snack.

Onion Rings

Serves: 4
Prep time: 15 minutes / Cook time: 8 minutes

Ingredients:
- 2 large onions, cut into rings
- 100g all-purpose flour
- 1 tsp paprika
- 1/2 tsp garlic powder
- 1/2 tsp onion powder
- Salt and black pepper, to taste
- 2 large eggs, beaten
- Breadcrumbs, for coating
- Vegetable oil, for frying

Preparation instructions:
1. Preheat the Ninja Dual Zone Air Fryer to 200°C on zone 1 for 5 minutes.
2. Separate the onion slices into rings.
3. In a shallow bowl, mix together the all-purpose flour, paprika, garlic powder, onion powder, salt, and black pepper.
4. Dip each onion ring into the beaten eggs, then coat it in the seasoned flour mixture, pressing gently to adhere.
5. Dip the coated onion ring back into the

beaten eggs, then roll it in breadcrumbs to coat thoroughly.
6. Place the coated onion rings in zone 1 of the air fryer, leaving space between them.
7. Cook the onion rings at 200°C for 6-8 minutes, or until they are golden and crispy.
8. Once cooked, remove the onion rings from the air fryer and let them cool for a minute before serving.
9. Serve the crunchy and flavorful onion rings as a tasty side dish or appetiser.

Crispy Fried Fish

Serves: 4
Prep time: 15 minutes / Cook time: 12 minutes

Ingredients:
- 500g white fish fillets (e.g., cod, haddock), cut into strips
- 100g all-purpose flour
- 1 tsp paprika
- 1/2 tsp garlic powder
- 1/2 tsp onion powder
- Salt and black pepper, to taste
- 2 large eggs, beaten
- Vegetable oil, for frying

Preparation instructions:
1. Preheat the Ninja Dual Zone Air Fryer to 200°C on zone 1 for 5 minutes.
2. In a shallow bowl, mix together the all-purpose flour, paprika, garlic powder, onion powder, salt, and black pepper.
3. Dip each fish strip into the beaten eggs, then coat it in the seasoned flour mixture, pressing gently to adhere.
4. Place the coated fish strips in zone 1 of the air fryer, leaving space between them.
5. Cook the fish at 200°C for 10-12 minutes, flipping them halfway through, or until they are golden brown and crispy.
6. Once cooked, remove the crispy fried fish from the air fryer and let it rest for a minute before serving.
7. Serve the delicious and crispy fried fish with tartar sauce, lemon wedges, or your favourite dipping sauce.

Cheesy Garlic Bread

Serves: 4
Prep time: 10 minutes / Cook time: 6 minutes

Ingredients:
- 1 baguette or loaf of bread
- 60g unsalted butter, softened
- 2 cloves of garlic, minced
- 1 tbsp chopped fresh parsley
- Salt, to taste
- 100g grated mozzarella cheese

Preparation instructions:
1. Preheat the Ninja Dual Zone Air Fryer to 200°C on zone 1 for 5 minutes.
2. Cut the baguette or loaf of bread into desired-sized slices.
3. In a small bowl, mix together the softened butter, minced garlic, chopped fresh parsley, and salt.
4. Spread the garlic butter mixture on one side of each bread slice.
5. Sprinkle the grated mozzarella cheese evenly on top of the garlic buttered slices.
6. Place the cheesy garlic bread slices in zone 1 of the air fryer.
7. Cook the garlic bread at 200°C for 4-6 minutes, or until the bread is toasted, the butter is melted, and the cheese is melted and bubbly.
8. Once cooked, remove the cheesy garlic bread from the air fryer and let it cool for a minute before serving.
9. Serve the flavorful and cheesy garlic bread as a delightful accompaniment to soups, salads, or as a snack.

Beef Taquitos

Serves: 4
Prep time: 15 minutes / Cook time: 10 minutes

Ingredients:
- 300g cooked shredded beef (e.g., leftover roast beef)
- 8 small flour tortillas
- 100g shredded cheddar cheese
- 1/2 tsp chilli powder
- 1/2 tsp cumin
- Salt and black pepper, to taste
- Vegetable oil, for brushing

Preparation instructions:
1. Preheat the Ninja Dual Zone Air Fryer to 200°C on zone 1 for 5 minutes.
2. In a bowl, combine the shredded beef, chilli powder, cumin, salt, and black pepper. Mix well.
3. Place a small amount of the seasoned shredded beef onto one end of each flour tortilla.
4. Sprinkle shredded cheddar cheese on top of the beef.
5. Roll up each tortilla tightly, securing the filling inside.
6. Brush the taquitos with vegetable oil to lightly coat them.
7. Place the taquitos in zone 1 of the air fryer, seam side down.
8. Cook the taquitos at 200°C for 8-10 minutes, or until they are golden brown and crispy.
9. Once cooked, remove the beef taquitos from the air fryer and let them cool for a minute.
10. Serve the tasty and handheld beef taquitos with salsa, guacamole, or sour cream for a flavorful Mexican-inspired dish.

Fish Sticks

Serves: 4
Prep time: 15 minutes / Cook time: 10 minutes

Ingredients:
- 500g white fish fillets (e.g., cod, haddock), cut into sticks
- 100g all-purpose flour
- 1 tsp paprika
- 1/2 tsp garlic powder
- 1/2 tsp onion powder
- Salt and black pepper, to taste
- 2 large eggs, beaten
- Breadcrumbs, for coating
- Vegetable oil, for frying

Preparation instructions:
1. Preheat the Ninja Dual Zone Air Fryer to 200°C on zone 1 for 5 minutes.
2. In a shallow bowl, mix together the all-purpose flour, paprika, garlic powder, onion powder, salt, and black pepper.
3. Dip each fish stick into the beaten eggs, then coat it in the seasoned flour mixture, pressing gently to adhere.
4. Dip the coated fish stick back into the beaten eggs, then roll it in breadcrumbs to coat thoroughly.
5. Place the coated fish sticks in zone 1 of the air fryer, leaving space between them.
6. Cook the fish sticks at 200°C for 8-10 minutes, flipping them halfway through, or until they are golden brown and crispy.
7. Once cooked, remove the fish sticks from the air fryer and let them rest for a minute before serving.
8. Serve the crispy and flavorful fish sticks with tartar sauce, ketchup, or your preferred dipping sauce for a delicious seafood treat.

Popcorn Chicken

Serves: 4
Prep time: 15 minutes / Cook time: 10 minutes

Ingredients:
- 500g boneless, skinless chicken breast, cut into bite-sized pieces
- 100g all-purpose flour
- 1 tsp paprika
- 1/2 tsp garlic powder
- 1/2 tsp onion powder
- Salt and black pepper, to taste
- 2 large eggs, beaten
- Breadcrumbs, for coating
- Vegetable oil, for frying

Preparation instructions:
1. Preheat the Ninja Dual Zone Air Fryer to 200°C on zone 1 for 5 minutes.
2. In a shallow bowl, mix together the all-purpose flour, paprika, garlic powder, onion powder, salt, and black pepper.
3. Dip each chicken piece into the beaten eggs, then coat it in the seasoned flour mixture, pressing gently to adhere.
4. Dip the coated chicken piece back into the beaten eggs, then roll it in breadcrumbs to coat thoroughly.
5. Place the coated popcorn chicken in zone 1 of the air fryer, leaving space between them.
6. Cook the popcorn chicken at 200°C for 8-10 minutes, flipping them halfway through, or until they are golden brown and crispy.
7. Once cooked, remove the popcorn chicken from the air fryer and let them rest for a minute before serving.
8. Serve the flavorful and bite-sized popcorn chicken with your favourite dipping sauce for a tasty snack or meal.

Buffalo Cauliflower

Serves: 4
Prep time: 15 minutes / Cook time: 12 minutes

Ingredients:
- 1 large cauliflower head, cut into florets
- 60g all-purpose flour
- 1 tsp paprika
- 1/2 tsp garlic powder
- 1/2 tsp onion powder
- Salt and black pepper, to taste
- 120ml milk
- 60ml hot sauce
- 30g unsalted butter, melted

Preparation instructions:
1. Preheat the Ninja Dual Zone Air Fryer to 200°C on zone 1 for 5 minutes.
2. In a bowl, whisk together the all-purpose flour, paprika, garlic powder, onion powder, salt, and black pepper.
3. In a separate bowl, mix the milk, hot sauce, and melted butter.
4. Dip each cauliflower floret into the milk mixture, allowing the excess to drip off.
5. Coat the cauliflower floret in the seasoned flour mixture, pressing gently to adhere.
6. Place the coated cauliflower florets in zone 1 of the air fryer, leaving space between them.
7. Cook the buffalo cauliflower at 200°C for 10-12 minutes, or until they are golden brown and crispy.
8. Once cooked, remove the buffalo cauliflower from the air fryer and let them cool for a minute.
9. Serve the tangy and spicy buffalo cauliflower as a flavorful appetisers or side dish.

Chicken Quesadillas

Serves: 4
Prep time: 15 minutes / Cook time: 8 minutes

Ingredients:
- 2 large chicken breasts, cooked and shredded
- 4 large flour tortillas
- 100g shredded cheddar cheese
- 1/2 tsp chilli powder
- 1/2 tsp cumin
- Salt and black pepper, to taste
- 2 tbsp chopped fresh cilantro
- Vegetable oil, for brushing

Preparation instructions:
1. Preheat the Ninja Dual Zone Air Fryer to 200°C on zone 1 for 5 minutes.
2. In a bowl, combine the shredded chicken, chilli powder, cumin, salt, black pepper, and chopped fresh cilantro. Mix well.
3. Place a tortilla on a flat surface and sprinkle shredded cheddar cheese on one half of the tortilla.
4. Spoon the seasoned shredded chicken mixture on top of the cheese.
5. Fold the tortilla in half to create a half-moon shape, pressing gently to seal.
6. Repeat the process with the remaining tortillas and filling ingredients.
7. Brush the quesadillas with vegetable oil to lightly coat them.
8. Place the quesadillas in zone 1 of the air fryer.
9. Cook the quesadillas at 200°C for 6-8 minutes, or until they are golden brown and the cheese is melted.
10. Once cooked, remove the chicken quesadillas from the air fryer and let them cool for a minute.
11. Serve the delicious and cheesy chicken quesadillas with salsa, guacamole, or sour cream for a satisfying meal.

Mini Pizzas

Serves: 4
Prep time: 15 minutes / Cook time: 10 minutes

Ingredients:
- 4 small pizza bases or English muffins, halved
- 200g pizza sauce or tomato sauce
- 200g shredded mozzarella cheese
- Toppings of your choice (e.g., sliced pepperoni, diced bell peppers, sliced mushrooms, olives)

Preparation instructions:
1. Preheat the Ninja Dual Zone Air Fryer to 200°C on zone 1 for 5 minutes.
2. Spread a generous amount of pizza sauce or tomato sauce on each pizza base or English muffin half.
3. Sprinkle shredded mozzarella cheese evenly on top of the sauce.
4. Add your favourite toppings, such as sliced pepperoni, diced bell peppers, sliced mushrooms, or olives.
5. Place the mini pizzas in zone 1 of the air fryer.
6. Cook the mini pizzas at 200°C for 8-10 minutes, or until the cheese is melted and bubbly, and the crust is golden brown.
7. Once cooked, remove the mini pizzas from the air fryer and let them cool for a minute.
8. Serve the mini pizzas as a fun and customizable meal or snack.

Jalapeno Poppers

Serves: 4
Prep time: 15 minutes / Cook time: 8 minutes

Ingredients:
- 8 large jalapeno peppers, halved lengthwise and seeded
- 100g cream cheese, softened

- 50g shredded cheddar cheese
- 1/4 tsp garlic powder
- Salt and black pepper, to taste
- 60g all-purpose flour
- 2 large eggs, beaten
- Breadcrumbs, for coating
- Vegetable oil, for frying

Preparation instructions:

1. Preheat the Ninja Dual Zone Air Fryer to 200°C on zone 1 for 5 minutes.
2. In a bowl, mix together the softened cream cheese, shredded cheddar cheese, garlic powder, salt, and black pepper until well combined.
3. Spoon the cream cheese mixture into each jalapeno half, filling them evenly.
4. In separate bowls, place the all-purpose flour, beaten eggs, and breadcrumbs.
5. Dip each stuffed jalapeno half into the flour, shaking off any excess.
6. Dip the floured jalapeno half into the beaten eggs, then roll it in breadcrumbs to coat thoroughly.
7. Place the coated jalapeno poppers in zone 1 of the air fryer, leaving space between them.
8. Cook the jalapeno poppers at 200°C for 6-8 minutes, or until they are golden brown and crispy.
9. Once cooked, remove the jalapeno poppers from the air fryer and let them cool for a minute.
10. Serve the delicious and spicy jalapeno poppers as a tasty appetiser or party snack.

Crab Cakes

Serves: 4

Prep time: 20 minutes / Cook time: 10 minutes

Ingredients:

- 250g crab meat, picked over for shells
- 50g breadcrumbs
- 30g mayonnaise
- 1 large egg, beaten
- 1 tbsp Dijon mustard
- 1 tbsp chopped fresh parsley
- 1/2 tsp Worcestershire sauce
- 1/4 tsp Old Bay seasoning (optional)
- Salt and black pepper, to taste
- Vegetable oil, for frying

Preparation instructions:

1. Preheat the Ninja Dual Zone Air Fryer to 200°C on zone 1 for 5 minutes.
2. In a bowl, combine the crab meat, breadcrumbs, mayonnaise, beaten egg, Dijon mustard, chopped fresh parsley, Worcestershire sauce, Old Bay seasoning (if using), salt, and black pepper. Mix well.
3. Form the crab mixture into patties, about 2-3 inches in diameter.
4. Place the crab cakes in zone 1 of the air fryer, leaving space between them.
5. Cook the crab cakes at 200°C for 8-10 minutes, flipping them halfway through, or until they are golden brown and cooked through.
6. Once cooked, remove the crab cakes from the air fryer and let them cool for a minute.
7. Serve the delicious and flavorful crab cakes as an appetiser or main dish, accompanied by tartar sauce or a squeeze of lemon juice.

Chapter 7: Appetisers

Crab Rangoon

Serves: 4
Prep time: 20 minutes / Cook time: 10 minutes

Ingredients:
- 200g cream cheese, softened
- 150g crab meat, picked over for shells
- 2 spring onions, finely chopped
- 1/2 tsp garlic powder
- 1/2 tsp Worcestershire sauce
- Salt and black pepper, to taste
- 16 wonton wrappers
- Vegetable oil, for frying

Preparation instructions:
1. Preheat the Ninja Dual Zone Air Fryer to 200°C on zone 1 for 5 minutes.
2. In a bowl, combine the softened cream cheese, crab meat, chopped spring onions, garlic powder, Worcestershire sauce, salt, and black pepper. Mix well.
3. Place a spoonful of the cream cheese and crab mixture in the centre of each wonton wrapper.
4. Moisten the edges of the wonton wrappers with water, then fold them over to create a triangle shape. Press the edges to seal.
5. Place the filled wontons in zone 1 of the air fryer, leaving space between them.
6. Cook the crab rangoon at 200°C for 8-10 minutes, or until they are golden brown and crispy.
7. Once cooked, remove the crab rangoon from the air fryer and let them cool for a minute.
8. Serve the delicious and creamy crab rangoon as an appetiser or party snack, accompanied by sweet chilli sauce or soy sauce for dipping.

Falafel Balls

Serves: 4
Prep time: 15 minutes / Cook time: 12 minutes

Ingredients:
- 200g dried chickpeas, soaked overnight and drained
- 1 small onion, chopped
- 2 cloves garlic, minced
- 2 tbsp chopped fresh parsley
- 2 tbsp chopped fresh coriander
- 1 tsp ground cumin
- 1 tsp ground coriander
- 1/2 tsp baking powder
- Salt and black pepper, to taste
- Vegetable oil, for brushing

Preparation instructions:
1. Preheat the Ninja Dual Zone Air Fryer to 200°C on zone 1 for 5 minutes.
2. In a food processor, combine the soaked and drained chickpeas, chopped onion, minced garlic, fresh parsley, fresh coriander, ground cumin, ground coriander, baking powder, salt, and black pepper. Process until a coarse mixture forms.
3. Shape the mixture into small balls, about 2-3 cm in diameter.
4. Place the falafel balls in zone 1 of the air fryer, leaving space between them.
5. Brush the falafel balls with vegetable oil to lightly coat them.
6. Cook the falafel balls at 200°C for 10-12 minutes, flipping them halfway through, or until they are golden brown and crispy.
7. Once cooked, remove the falafel balls from the air fryer and let them cool for a minute.
8. Serve the delicious and flavorful falafel balls as a vegetarian appetiser or in pita bread with tahini sauce and fresh vegetables.

Loaded Potato Skins

Serves: 4

Prep time: 15 minutes / Cook time: 20 minutes

Ingredients:
- 4 large potatoes
- 100g shredded cheddar cheese
- 4 slices bacon, cooked and crumbled
- 2 spring onions, finely chopped
- 60ml sour cream
- Salt and black pepper, to taste

Preparation instructions:
1. Preheat the Ninja Dual Zone Air Fryer to 200°C on zone 1 for 5 minutes.
2. Pierce the potatoes several times with a fork, then place them in zone 1 of the air fryer.
3. Cook the potatoes at 200°C for 20 minutes, or until they are cooked through and tender.
4. Once cooked, remove the potatoes from the air fryer and let them cool slightly.
5. Cut each potato in half lengthwise, then scoop out the flesh, leaving a thin layer attached to the skins.
6. In a bowl, mix together the shredded cheddar cheese, crumbled bacon, chopped spring onions, sour cream, salt, and black pepper.
7. Spoon the cheese and bacon mixture into the hollowed-out potato skins, filling them generously.
8. Place the loaded potato skins in zone 1 of the air fryer, leaving space between them.
9. Cook the loaded potato skins at 200°C for 6-8 minutes, or until the cheese is melted and bubbly.
10. Once cooked, remove the loaded potato skins from the air fryer and let them cool for a minute.
11. Serve the loaded potato skins as a delicious appetisers or side dish, garnished with additional sour cream and spring onions, if desired.

Fried Pickles

Serves: 4

Prep time: 15 minutes / Cook time: 8 minutes

Ingredients:
- 200g pickles, sliced into thin rounds
- 100g all-purpose flour
- 2 large eggs, beaten
- 100g breadcrumbs
- 1/2 tsp paprika
- 1/2 tsp garlic powder
- Salt and black pepper, to taste
- Vegetable oil, for frying

Preparation instructions:
1. Preheat the Ninja Dual Zone Air Fryer to 200°C on zone 1 for 5 minutes.
2. In a shallow dish, combine the all-purpose flour, paprika, garlic powder, salt, and black pepper.
3. Dip each pickle slice into the flour mixture, shaking off any excess.
4. Dip the floured pickle slice into the beaten eggs, then roll it in breadcrumbs to coat thoroughly.
5. Place the coated pickles in zone 1 of the air fryer, leaving space between them.
6. Cook the fried pickles at 200°C for 6-8 minutes, or until they are golden brown and crispy.
7. Once cooked, remove the fried pickles from the air fryer and let them cool for a minute.
8. Serve the crispy and tangy fried pickles as a tasty appetiser or snack, accompanied by ranch dressing or your favourite dipping sauce.

Panko Crusted Shrimp

Serves: 4

Prep time: 15 minutes / Cook time: 8 minutes

Ingredients:
- 300g large shrimp, peeled and deveined

- 100g all-purpose flour
- 2 large eggs, beaten
- 150g panko breadcrumbs
- 1/2 tsp paprika
- 1/2 tsp garlic powder
- Salt and black pepper, to taste
- Vegetable oil, for frying

Preparation instructions:

1. Preheat the Ninja Dual Zone Air Fryer to 200°C on zone 1 for 5 minutes.
2. In a shallow dish, combine the all-purpose flour, paprika, garlic powder, salt, and black pepper.
3. Dip each shrimp into the flour mixture, shaking off any excess.
4. Dip the floured shrimp into the beaten eggs, then roll it in panko breadcrumbs to coat thoroughly.
5. Place the coated shrimp in zone 1 of the air fryer, leaving space between them.
6. Cook the panko crusted shrimp at 200°C for 6-8 minutes, or until they are golden brown and crispy.
7. Once cooked, remove the panko crusted shrimp from the air fryer and let them cool for a minute.
8. Serve the crunchy and flavorful panko crusted shrimp as an appetiser or main dish, accompanied by a dipping sauce of your choice.

Spinach and Feta Stuffed Mushrooms

Serves: 4
Prep time: 15 minutes / Cook time: 12 minutes

Ingredients:

- 16 large mushrooms
- 200g fresh spinach, chopped
- 100g feta cheese, crumbled
- 1 small onion, finely chopped
- 2 cloves garlic, minced
- 1 tbsp olive oil
- Salt and black pepper, to taste

Preparation instructions:

1. Preheat the Ninja Dual Zone Air Fryer to 200°C on zone 1 for 5 minutes.
2. Remove the stems from the mushrooms and set them aside.
3. In a skillet, heat the olive oil over medium heat. Add the chopped mushroom stems, onion, and minced garlic. Cook until the onion is translucent and the mushroom stems are tender.
4. Add the chopped spinach to the skillet and cook until wilted. Remove from heat and let the mixture cool slightly.
5. In a bowl, combine the cooked spinach mixture and crumbled feta cheese. Season with salt and black pepper, to taste.
6. Spoon the spinach and feta mixture into the mushroom caps, filling them generously.
7. Place the stuffed mushrooms in zone 1 of the air fryer, leaving space between them.
8. Cook the stuffed mushrooms at 200°C for 10-12 minutes, or until the mushrooms are tender and the filling is heated through.
9. Once cooked, remove the stuffed mushrooms from the air fryer and let them cool for a minute.
10. Serve the savoury and cheesy spinach and feta stuffed mushrooms as an appetiser or side dish.

Coconut Chicken Strips

Serves: 4
Prep time: 20 minutes / Cook time: 10 minutes

Ingredients:

- 400g chicken breast, cut into strips
- 100g all-purpose flour
- 2 large eggs, beaten
- 100g shredded coconut

- 1/2 tsp paprika
- 1/2 tsp garlic powder
- Salt and black pepper, to taste
- Vegetable oil, for frying

Preparation instructions:
1. Preheat the Ninja Dual Zone Air Fryer to 200°C on zone 1 for 5 minutes.
2. In a shallow dish, combine the all-purpose flour, paprika, garlic powder, salt, and black pepper.
3. Dip each chicken strip into the flour mixture, shaking off any excess.
4. Dip the floured chicken strip into the beaten eggs, then roll it in shredded coconut to coat thoroughly.
5. Place the coated chicken strips in zone 1 of the air fryer, leaving space between them.
6. Cook the coconut chicken strips at 200°C for 8-10 minutes, or until they are golden brown and cooked through.
7. Once cooked, remove the coconut chicken strips from the air fryer and let them cool for a minute.
8. Serve the crispy and tropical-flavoured coconut chicken strips as a delicious appetisers or main dish, accompanied by sweet chilli sauce or a dipping sauce of your choice.

Greek Feta Fries

Serves: 4
Prep time: 15 minutes / Cook time: 20 minutes

Ingredients:
- 4 large potatoes, cut into fries
- 2 tbsp olive oil
- 100g feta cheese, crumbled
- 2 tbsp chopped fresh parsley
- 1 tsp dried oregano
- Salt and black pepper, to taste

Preparation instructions:
1. Preheat the Ninja Dual Zone Air Fryer to 200°C on zone 1 for 5 minutes.
2. In a bowl, toss the potato fries with olive oil to coat them evenly.
3. Place the potato fries in zone 1 of the air fryer, spreading them out in a single layer.
4. Cook the fries at 200°C for 18-20 minutes, shaking the basket or flipping the fries halfway through, or until they are golden brown and crispy.
5. Once cooked, remove the fries from the air fryer and let them cool slightly.
6. In a separate bowl, combine the crumbled feta cheese, chopped fresh parsley, dried oregano, salt, and black pepper.
7. Sprinkle the feta cheese mixture over the hot fries, allowing it to melt slightly.
8. Serve the flavorful and cheesy Greek feta fries as a delicious side dish or snack, garnished with additional parsley, if desired.

Zucchini Fritters

Serves: 4
Prep time: 15 minutes / Cook time: 12 minutes

Ingredients:
- 2 large zucchinis, grated and squeezed to remove excess moisture
- 1 small onion, grated
- 2 cloves garlic, minced
- 2 eggs, beaten
- 60g all-purpose flour
- 2 tbsp chopped fresh dill
- Salt and black pepper, to taste
- Vegetable oil, for frying

Preparation instructions:
1. Preheat the Ninja Dual Zone Air Fryer to 200°C on zone 1 for 5 minutes.
2. In a bowl, combine the grated and squeezed zucchinis, grated onion, minced garlic, beaten eggs, all-purpose flour, chopped fresh dill, salt, and black pepper. Mix well.

3. Form the zucchini mixture into small patties, about 5 cm in diameter.
4. Place the zucchini fritters in zone 1 of the air fryer, leaving space between them.
5. Cook the fritters at 200°C for 10-12 minutes, flipping them halfway through, or until they are golden brown and crispy.
6. Once cooked, remove the zucchini fritters from the air fryer and let them cool for a minute.
7. Serve the delicious and healthy zucchini fritters as a side dish or appetiser, accompanied by tzatziki sauce or a yoghurt-based dip.

Vietnamese Spring Rolls

Serves: 4
Prep time: 30 minutes / Cook time: 8 minutes

Ingredients:
- 8 rice paper wrappers
- 200g cooked shrimp, peeled and deveined
- 100g rice vermicelli noodles, cooked and drained
- 1 carrot, cut into matchstick strips
- 1/2 cucumber, cut into matchstick strips
- 4 leaves lettuce, torn into smaller pieces
- Fresh mint leaves
- Fresh cilantro leaves
- Dipping sauce (such as hoisin sauce or peanut sauce)

Preparation instructions:
1. Preheat the Ninja Dual Zone Air Fryer to 200°C on zone 1 for 5 minutes.
2. Fill a shallow dish with warm water. Dip a rice paper wrapper into the water for a few seconds until it becomes pliable, then place it on a clean surface.
3. On one edge of the rice paper wrapper, place a few cooked shrimp, a small handful of cooked rice vermicelli noodles, matchstick strips of carrot and cucumber, torn lettuce leaves, fresh mint leaves, and fresh cilantro leaves.
4. Roll the edge with the filling over once, tucking it in tightly. Fold in the sides of the wrapper, then continue rolling it up tightly until it forms a spring roll.
5. Repeat the process with the remaining rice paper wrappers and filling ingredients.
6. Place the spring rolls in zone 1 of the air fryer, leaving space between them.
7. Cook the spring rolls at 200°C for 6-8 minutes, or until they are crispy and lightly browned.
8. Once cooked, remove the spring rolls from the air fryer and let them cool for a minute.
9. Serve the fresh and flavorful Vietnamese spring rolls as a healthy appetisers or light meal, accompanied by your favourite dipping sauce.

Caprese Stuffed Mushrooms

Serves: 4
Prep time: 15 minutes / Cook time: 12 minutes

Ingredients:
- 16 large mushrooms
- 200g fresh mozzarella, diced
- 4 ripe tomatoes, diced
- 30g chopped fresh basil
- 2 tbsp balsamic glaze
- Salt and black pepper, to taste

Preparation instructions:
1. Preheat the Ninja Dual Zone Air Fryer to 200°C on zone 1 for 5 minutes.
2. Remove the stems from the mushrooms and set them aside.
3. In a bowl, combine the diced mozzarella, diced tomatoes, chopped fresh basil, balsamic glaze, salt, and black pepper. Mix well.
4. Spoon the caprese mixture into the mushroom caps, filling them generously.

5. Place the stuffed mushrooms in zone 1 of the air fryer, leaving space between them.
6. Cook the stuffed mushrooms at 200°C for 10-12 minutes, or until the mushrooms are tender and the filling is heated through.
7. Once cooked, remove the stuffed mushrooms from the air fryer and let them cool for a minute.
8. Serve the delightful and flavorful caprese stuffed mushrooms as an appetiser or side dish, garnished with additional fresh basil, if desired.

Pork Dumplings

Serves: 4
Prep time: 30 minutes / Cook time: 12 minutes

Ingredients:
- 250g ground pork
- 30g finely chopped cabbage
- 2 green onions, finely chopped
- 2 cloves garlic, minced
- 1 tsp grated fresh ginger
- 1 tbsp soy sauce
- 1 tbsp sesame oil
- 1/2 tsp sugar
- 1/4 tsp black pepper
- 24 round dumpling wrappers
- Water, for sealing
- Vegetable oil, for frying

Preparation instructions:
1. Preheat the Ninja Dual Zone Air Fryer to 200°C on zone 1 for 5 minutes.
2. In a bowl, combine the ground pork, chopped cabbage, chopped green onions, minced garlic, grated fresh ginger, soy sauce, sesame oil, sugar, and black pepper. Mix well.
3. Place a small spoonful of the pork filling in the centre of a dumpling wrapper. Moisten the edges of the wrapper with water, then fold it in half and seal the edges, crimping them to create a pleated appearance. Repeat with the remaining wrappers and filling.
4. Place the dumplings in zone 1 of the air fryer, leaving space between them.
5. Cook the pork dumplings at 200°C for 10-12 minutes, or until they are golden brown and cooked through.
6. Once cooked, remove the pork dumplings from the air fryer and let them cool for a minute.
7. Serve the savoury and satisfying pork dumplings as an appetiser or main dish, accompanied by soy sauce or your favourite dipping sauce.

Double Bean Chilli

Serves 8
Prep time: 10 minutes / Cook time: 20 minutes

Ingredients
- 2 tbsp rapeseed oil
- 2 medium onions, chopped
- 1 large carrot, chopped
- 2 bell peppers, seeded and chopped
- 2 tsp chipotle paste
- 1 tbsp dried oregano
- 1 tbsp ground coriander
- 1 bay leaf
- 2 (400g) cans tomatoes, crushed
- 4 (400g) cans kidney beans, drained and rinsed
- 1 (400g) can refried beans

Preparation Instructions
1. Heat 1 tablespoon of rapeseed oil in a sauté pan over medium-high heat. Once hot, sauté the onion, carrot, and peppers for about 4 minutes, until just tender.
2. Brush the inside of two oven-safe baking tins with olive oil. Thoroughly combine all the ingredients.
3. Spoon the mixture into the baking tins and add them to the drawers.

4. Select zone 1 and pair it with "AIR FRY" at 180°C for 20 minutes. Select "MATCH" to duplicate settings across both zones. Press the "START/STOP" button.
5. When zone 1 time reaches 10 minutes, stir the beans, and reinsert the drawers to continue cooking.

Aubergine Burgers

Serves 4
Prep time: 10 minutes / Cook time: 15 minutes

Ingredients
- 1 large aubergine, wide middle section cut into 8 rounds
- 1 tbsp olive oil
- 1 tsp stone-ground mustard
- 1/2 tsp ground cumin
- Sea salt and ground black pepper, to taste
- 8 tbsp breadcrumbs
- 8 ciabatta rolls, halved
- 8 tbsp tofu mayonnaise
- 8 leaves Romaine lettuce
- 1 medium tomato, sliced
- 1 onion, sliced

Preparation Instructions
1. Insert crisper plates in both drawers. Spray the crisper plates with nonstick cooking oil.
2. Toss the aubergine rounds with olive oil, mustard, cumin, salt, black pepper, and breadcrumbs. Toss until they are well coated on all sides.
3. Select zone 1 and pair it with "AIR FRY" at 200°C for 15 minutes. Select "MATCH" followed by the "START/STOP" button.
4. Turn over aubergine rounds halfway through the cooking time to ensure even cooking.
5. Lastly, spread the rolls with tofu mayonnaise. Top the rolls with fried aubergine rounds, lettuce, tomato, and onion slices. Serve immediately and enjoy!

Cheesy Polenta Stacks

Serves 6
Prep time: 10 minutes / Cook time: 30minutes

Ingredients
- 350ml vegetable broth
- 150g quick-cook polenta
- 2 tsp soy butter
- Sea salt and ground black pepper, to taste
- 1 tsp cayenne pepper
- 150g cheddar cheese, sliced

Preparation Instructions
1. In a saucepan, bring the vegetable broth to a rapid boil. Immediately turn the heat to a medium-low; gradually and carefully, stir in the polenta, butter, salt, black pepper, and cayenne pepper.
2. Let it simmer, for about 5 minutes, uncovered, whisking continuously to avoid lumps. Pour your polenta into a deep baking tray and let it cool completely.
3. Then, transfer the baking tray to your fridge until well-chilled. Once the polenta is chilled, cut it into squares, using a sharp oiled knife.
4. Insert the crisper plates in both drawers and spray them with cooking oil. Arrange polenta squares on the crisper plates.
5. Select zone 1 and pair it with "AIR FRY" at 190°C for 30 minutes. Select "MATCH" to duplicate settings across both zones. Press the "START/STOP" button.
6. When zone 1 time reaches 10 minutes, turn the polenta squares over and brush them with nonstick cooking oil; reinsert the drawers to continue cooking.
7. When zone 1 time reaches 20 minutes, turn the polenta squares over and top them with cheese slices; reinsert the drawers to continue cooking.

Chapter 8: Snacks and Desserts

Strawberry Cheesecake Egg Rolls

Serves: 4
Prep time: 15 minutes / Cook time: 8 minutes

Ingredients:
- 8 egg roll wrappers
- 200g cream cheese, softened
- 50g powdered sugar
- 1 tsp vanilla extract
- 150g fresh strawberries, diced
- Vegetable oil, for frying
- Icing sugar, for dusting

Preparation instructions:
1. Preheat the Ninja Dual Zone Air Fryer to 190°C in zone 1 for 5 minutes.
2. In a bowl, combine the softened cream cheese, powdered sugar, and vanilla extract. Mix well until smooth and creamy.
3. Lay an egg roll wrapper on a clean surface. Spoon a tablespoon of the cream cheese mixture onto one corner of the wrapper.
4. Place a few pieces of diced strawberries on top of the cream cheese mixture.
5. Fold the sides of the wrapper over the filling, then roll it up tightly into an egg roll shape, sealing the edges with a bit of water.
6. Repeat the process with the remaining egg roll wrappers and filling ingredients.
7. Place the strawberry cheesecake egg rolls in zone 1 of the air fryer, leaving space between them.
8. Cook the egg rolls at 190°C for 6-8 minutes, or until they are golden brown and crispy.
9. Once cooked, remove the egg rolls from the air fryer and let them cool for a minute.
10. Dust the strawberry cheesecake egg rolls with icing sugar before serving. Enjoy them warm as a delightful dessert or snack.

Mini Apple Pies

Serves: 4
Prep time: 20 minutes / Cook time: 12 minutes

Ingredients:
- 2 apples, peeled, cored, and diced
- 50g granulated sugar
- 1/2 tsp ground cinnamon
- 1/4 tsp ground nutmeg
- 1 tbsp lemon juice
- 8 small pre-made pie crusts
- 2 tbsp unsalted butter, melted
- Icing sugar, for dusting

Preparation instructions:
1. Preheat the Ninja Dual Zone Air Fryer to 190°C in zone 1 for 5 minutes.
2. In a bowl, combine the diced apples, granulated sugar, ground cinnamon, ground nutmeg, and lemon juice. Mix well to coat the apples with the sugar and spices.
3. Roll out the pie crusts and cut them into smaller circles to fit your silicone muffin cups.
4. Press each pie crust circle into a silicone muffin cup, forming a small pie shell.
5. Fill each pie shell with the apple mixture, dividing it evenly among the cups.
6. Brush the melted butter over the top of each mini apple pie.
7. Place the mini apple pies in zone 1 of the air fryer, leaving space between them.
8. Cook the pies at 190°C for 10-12 minutes, or until the crust is golden brown and the apples are tender.
9. Once cooked, remove the mini apple pies from the air fryer and let them cool for a minute.
10. Dust the pies with icing sugar before serving. Enjoy these individual-sized apple

pies as a delicious dessert, served warm with a scoop of vanilla ice cream.

S'mores

Serves: 4
Prep time: 5 minutes / Cook time: 5 minutes

Ingredients:
- 8 graham crackers, broken in half
- 4 large marshmallows
- 50g milk chocolate, broken into pieces

Preparation instructions:
1. Preheat the Ninja Dual Zone Air Fryer to 190°C in zone 1 for 5 minutes.
2. Place 4 graham cracker halves on a clean surface.
3. Place a marshmallow on top of each graham cracker half.
4. Top each marshmallow with a few pieces of milk chocolate.
5. Place the remaining graham cracker halves on top to form a sandwich.
6. Place the s'mores in zone 1 of the air fryer, leaving space between them.
7. Cook the s'mores at 190°C for 4-5 minutes, or until the marshmallows are melted and gooey.
8. Once cooked, remove the s'mores from the air fryer and let them cool for a minute.
9. Serve the warm and gooey s'mores as a classic campfire treat. Enjoy!

Blueberry Hand Pies

Serves: 4
Prep time: 15 minutes / Cook time: 12 minutes

Ingredients:
- 200g fresh blueberries
- 50g granulated sugar
- 1 tbsp cornstarch
- 1 tsp lemon juice
- 8 small pre-made pie crusts
- 2 tbsp unsalted butter, melted
- Icing sugar, for dusting

Preparation instructions:
1. Preheat the Ninja Dual Zone Air Fryer to 190°C in zone 1 for 5 minutes.
2. In a bowl, combine the fresh blueberries, granulated sugar, cornstarch, and lemon juice. Gently mix until the blueberries are coated.
3. Roll out the pie crusts and cut them into smaller circles to fit your silicone muffin cups.
4. Press each pie crust circle into a silicone muffin cup, forming a small pie shell.
5. Fill each pie shell with the blueberry mixture, dividing it evenly among the cups.
6. Brush the melted butter over the top of each hand pie.
7. Place the hand pies in zone 1 of the air fryer, leaving space between them.
8. Cook the pies at 190°C for 10-12 minutes, or until the crust is golden brown and the blueberries are bubbling.
9. Once cooked, remove the hand pies from the air fryer and let them cool for a minute.
10. Dust the pies with icing sugar before serving. Enjoy these handheld blueberry pies as a delightful dessert or snack.

Nutella-Stuffed French Toast

Serves: 4
Prep time: 10 minutes / Cook time: 8 minutes

Ingredients:
- 8 slices of bread
- Nutella, for spreading
- 2 large eggs
- 120ml milk
- 1 tsp vanilla extract
- Butter, for cooking

- Maple syrup, for serving
- Fresh berries, for garnish (optional)

Preparation instructions:
1. Preheat the Ninja Dual Zone Air Fryer to 180°C on zone 1 for 5 minutes.
2. Spread Nutella on 4 slices of bread and top them with the remaining 4 slices to form sandwiches.
3. In a shallow dish, whisk together the eggs, milk, and vanilla extract until well combined.
4. Dip each Nutella sandwich into the egg mixture, allowing it to soak for a few seconds on each side.
5. Heat a small amount of butter in a non-stick frying pan over medium heat.
6. Place the soaked Nutella sandwiches in the pan and cook for 2-3 minutes on each side, or until golden brown and crispy.
7. Once cooked, transfer the French toast to zone 2 of the air fryer and cook at 180°C for an additional 3-5 minutes to ensure the centre is warm and the toast is fully cooked.
8. Once done, remove the Nutella-stuffed French toast from the air fryer and let them cool for a minute.
9. Serve the French toast warm with a drizzle of maple syrup and fresh berries, if desired. Enjoy this indulgent breakfast or brunch treat!

Chocolate Lava Cakes

Serves: 4
Prep time: 10 minutes / Cook time: 12 minutes

Ingredients:
- 100g dark chocolate
- 100g unsalted butter
- 2 large eggs
- 60g granulated sugar
- 30g all-purpose flour
- Pinch of salt
- Cooking spray or extra butter, for greasing
- Icing sugar, for dusting
- Fresh berries, for garnish (optional)

Preparation instructions:
1. Preheat the Ninja Dual Zone Air Fryer to 180°C on zone 1 for 5 minutes.
2. In a microwave-safe bowl, melt the dark chocolate and butter together in short bursts, stirring in between, until smooth. Let it cool slightly.
3. In a separate bowl, whisk the eggs and granulated sugar together until well combined.
4. Gradually add the melted chocolate mixture to the egg mixture, whisking constantly.
5. Sift in the flour and salt, and gently fold until just combined.
6. Grease 4 ramekins or silicone muffin cups with cooking spray or butter.
7. Divide the batter evenly among the greased ramekins or cups.
8. Place the ramekins or cups in zone 1 of the air fryer and cook at 180°C for 12 minutes or until the edges are set but the centres are still slightly gooey.
9. Once cooked, remove the lava cakes from the air fryer and let them cool for a minute.
10. Carefully invert the cakes onto serving plates and dust with icing sugar. Garnish with fresh berries if desired. Serve immediately and enjoy the rich and decadent chocolate lava cakes.

Peanut Butter Cupcakes

Serves: 4
Prep time: 15 minutes / Cook time: 20 minutes

Ingredients:
- 80g all-purpose flour
- 60g granulated sugar
- 1/2 tsp baking powder

- 1/4 tsp salt
- 30g unsalted butter, softened
- 60ml whole milk
- 1 large egg
- 1/2 tsp vanilla extract
- 4 tbsp creamy peanut butter
- Peanut butter chips, for garnish (optional)

Preparation instructions:
1. Preheat the Ninja Dual Zone Air Fryer to 180°C on zone 1 for 5 minutes.
2. In a bowl, whisk together the flour, granulated sugar, baking powder, and salt.
3. Add the softened butter, milk, egg, and vanilla extract to the dry ingredients. Mix until well combined.
4. Line 4 cupcake moulds or silicone muffin cups with cupcake liners.
5. Fill each liner halfway with the cupcake batter.
6. Place 1 tablespoon of creamy peanut butter on top of the batter in each liner.
7. Spoon the remaining cupcake batter over the peanut butter, covering it completely.
8. Sprinkle peanut butter chips on top for added flavour and texture, if desired.
9. Place the cupcake moulds or cups in zone 1 of the air fryer and cook at 180°C for 20 minutes or until a toothpick inserted into the centre comes out clean.
10. Once cooked, remove the peanut butter cupcakes from the air fryer and let them cool for a minute.
11. Serve the cupcakes as is or frost them with peanut butter frosting for extra indulgence. Enjoy these delightful peanut butter treats!

Lemon Bars

Serves: 4
Prep time: 15 minutes / Cook time: 25 minutes

Ingredients:
- 120g unsalted butter, softened
- 50g powdered sugar
- 160g all-purpose flour
- 2 large eggs
- 200g granulated sugar
- 30g all-purpose flour
- 1/2 tsp baking powder
- Zest of 1 lemon
- Juice of 1 lemon
- Powdered sugar, for dusting

Preparation instructions:
1. Preheat the Ninja Dual Zone Air Fryer to 180°C on zone 1 for 5 minutes.
2. In a bowl, cream together the softened butter and powdered sugar until light and fluffy.
3. Add the flour and mix until crumbly.
4. Press the mixture evenly into the bottom of a greased baking dish or silicone baking mould.
5. In another bowl, whisk together the eggs, granulated sugar, flour, baking powder, lemon zest, and lemon juice until well combined.
6. Pour the lemon mixture over the crust in the baking dish or mould.
7. Place the baking dish or mould in zone 1 of the air fryer and cook at 180°C for 25 minutes or until the edges are golden brown and the centre is set.
8. Once cooked, remove the lemon bars from the air fryer and let them cool completely.
9. Dust the bars with powdered sugar before serving. Cut into squares and enjoy the tangy and sweet lemon bars.

Peach Cobbler

Serves: 4
Prep time: 15 minutes / Cook time: 25 minutes

Ingredients:
- 4 large peaches, peeled and sliced
- 80g granulated sugar

- 1 tbsp lemon juice
- 1/2 tsp ground cinnamon
- 60g all-purpose flour
- 50g unsalted butter, melted
- 60ml whole milk
- 1/2 tsp vanilla extract
- Whipped cream or vanilla ice cream, for serving (optional)

Preparation instructions:
1. Preheat the Ninja Dual Zone Air Fryer to 180°C on zone 1 for 5 minutes.
2. In a bowl, combine the sliced peaches, granulated sugar, lemon juice, and ground cinnamon. Mix well.
3. In a separate bowl, whisk together the flour, melted butter, milk, and vanilla extract until smooth.
4. Grease a baking dish or silicone baking mould.
5. Pour the peach mixture into the greased dish or mould.
6. Pour the batter mixture over the peaches, spreading it evenly.
7. Place the baking dish or mould in zone 1 of the air fryer and cook at 180°C for 25 minutes or until the cobbler topping is golden brown and the peaches are tender.
8. Once cooked, remove the peach cobbler from the air fryer and let it cool for a few minutes.
9. Serve the cobbler warm, optionally topped with whipped cream or vanilla ice cream. Enjoy the comforting and fruity dessert!

Banana Bread

Serves: 4
Prep time: 15 minutes / Cook time: 35 minutes

Ingredients:
- 3 ripe bananas, mashed
- 80g unsalted butter, melted
- 100g granulated sugar
- 1 large egg
- 1 tsp vanilla extract
- 160g all-purpose flour
- 1/2 tsp baking soda
- 1/4 tsp salt
- 1/2 tsp ground cinnamon
- Chopped walnuts or chocolate chips (optional)

Preparation instructions:
1. Preheat the Ninja Dual Zone Air Fryer to 160°C on zone 1 for 5 minutes.
2. In a bowl, mix together the mashed bananas, melted butter, granulated sugar, egg, and vanilla extract until well combined.
3. In a separate bowl, whisk together the flour, baking soda, salt, and ground cinnamon.
4. Gradually add the dry ingredients to the banana mixture, stirring until just combined. Do not overmix.
5. Fold in the chopped walnuts or chocolate chips, if using.
6. Grease a loaf pan or silicone baking mould.
7. Pour the batter into the greased pan or mould, spreading it evenly.
8. Place the pan or mould in zone 1 of the air fryer and cook at 160°C for 35 minutes or until a toothpick inserted into the centre comes out clean.
9. Once cooked, remove the banana bread from the air fryer and let it cool in the pan or mould for a few minutes.
10. Transfer the banana bread to a wire rack to cool completely before slicing. Enjoy the moist and flavorful banana bread as a delightful snack or breakfast treat.

Cherry Turnovers

Serves: 4
Prep time: 15 minutes / Cook time: 15 minutes

Ingredients:
- 200g puff pastry, thawed

- 200g cherry pie filling
- 1 large egg, beaten
- 1 tbsp milk
- Icing sugar, for dusting

Preparation instructions:
1. Preheat the Ninja Dual Zone Air Fryer to 180°C on zone 1 for 5 minutes.
2. Roll out the puff pastry on a lightly floured surface into a square or rectangle, about 3mm thick.
3. Cut the pastry into 4 equal squares or rectangles.
4. Place a spoonful of cherry pie filling on one half of each pastry square or rectangle, leaving a border around the edges.
5. Fold the other half of the pastry over the filling, forming a triangle or rectangle shape.
6. Use a fork to crimp the edges of the turnovers, sealing them.
7. In a small bowl, whisk together the beaten egg and milk to make an egg wash.
8. Brush the tops of the turnovers with the egg wash.
9. Place the turnovers in zone 1 of the air fryer and cook at 180°C for 15 minutes or until the pastry is golden brown and puffed.
10. Once cooked, remove the cherry turnovers from the air fryer and let them cool for a few minutes.
11. Dust the turnovers with icing sugar before serving. Enjoy the flaky and fruity cherry turnovers as a delightful dessert or snack.

Bread Pudding with Caramel Sauce

Serves: 4
Prep time: 15 minutes / Cook time: 30 minutes

Ingredients:
- 4 slices day-old bread, cubed
- 300ml whole milk
- 2 large eggs
- 80g granulated sugar
- 1 tsp vanilla extract
- 1/2 tsp ground cinnamon
- Pinch of salt
- Caramel sauce, for serving

Preparation instructions:
1. Preheat the Ninja Dual Zone Air Fryer to 180°C on zone 1 for 5 minutes.
2. In a bowl, combine the bread cubes and milk, allowing the bread to soak for a few minutes.
3. In another bowl, whisk together the eggs, granulated sugar, vanilla extract, ground cinnamon, and salt.
4. Pour the egg mixture over the soaked bread cubes, stirring gently to combine.
5. Grease a baking dish or silicone baking mould.
6. Transfer the bread mixture to the greased dish or mould, spreading it evenly.
7. Place the dish or mould in zone 1 of the air fryer and cook at 180°C for 30 minutes or until the top is golden brown and the pudding is set.
8. Once cooked, remove the bread pudding from the air fryer and let it cool for a few minutes.
9. Serve the bread pudding warm, drizzled with caramel sauce. Enjoy the comforting and indulgent dessert!

Mini Cheesecakes

Serves: 4
Prep time: 15 minutes / Cook time: 20 minutes

Ingredients:
- 150g digestive biscuits, crushed
- 60g unsalted butter, melted
- 200g cream cheese
- 80g granulated sugar

- 1 large egg
- 1/2 tsp vanilla extract
- Fresh berries, for garnish (optional)

Preparation instructions:
1. Preheat the Ninja Dual Zone Air Fryer to 160°C on zone 1 for 5 minutes.
2. In a bowl, mix the crushed digestive biscuits and melted butter until well combined.
3. Line 4 cupcake moulds or silicone muffin cups with cupcake liners.
4. Divide the biscuit mixture among the cupcake liners, pressing it firmly into the bottom to form the crust.
5. In another bowl, beat the cream cheese, granulated sugar, egg, and vanilla extract until smooth and creamy.
6. Spoon the cream cheese mixture over the biscuit crust in each cupcake liner, filling them almost to the top.
7. Place the cupcake moulds or cups in zone 1 of the air fryer and cook at 160°C for 20 minutes or until the edges are set and the centres are slightly jiggly.
8. Once cooked, remove the mini cheesecakes from the air fryer and let them cool in the moulds or cups for a few minutes.
9. Transfer the cheesecakes to a wire rack to cool completely.
10. Before serving, garnish with fresh berries if desired. Enjoy these creamy and delicious mini cheesecakes as an elegant dessert.

Pumpkin Spice Donut Holes

Serves: 4
Prep time: 15 minutes / Cook time: 10 minutes

Ingredients:
- 150g all-purpose flour
- 80g granulated sugar
- 1 tsp baking powder
- 1/2 tsp ground cinnamon
- 1/4 tsp ground nutmeg
- 1/4 tsp ground cloves
- 1/4 tsp salt
- 60g pumpkin puree
- 60ml milk
- 1 large egg
- 1 tsp vanilla extract
- Icing sugar, for dusting

Preparation instructions:
1. Preheat the Ninja Dual Zone Air Fryer to 180°C on zone 1 for 5 minutes.
2. In a bowl, whisk together the flour, granulated sugar, baking powder, ground cinnamon, ground nutmeg, ground cloves, and salt.
3. In another bowl, mix together the pumpkin puree, milk, egg, and vanilla extract until well combined.
4. Gradually add the wet ingredients to the dry ingredients, stirring until just combined. Do not overmix.
5. Grease your hands with a little oil or butter.
6. Take small portions of the dough and roll them into small balls, creating donut holes.
7. Place the donut holes in zone 1 of the air fryer and cook at 180°C for 10 minutes or until golden brown and cooked through.
8. Once cooked, remove the pumpkin spice donut holes from the air fryer and let them cool for a minute.
9. Dust the donut holes with icing sugar before serving. Enjoy these bite-sized treats with the warm and comforting flavours of pumpkin spice.

Almond Biscotti

Serves: 4
Prep time: 15 minutes / Cook time: 25 minutes

Ingredients:
- 180g all-purpose flour
- 120g granulated sugar

- 1/2 tsp baking powder
- 1/4 tsp salt
- 2 large eggs
- 1/2 tsp almond extract
- 60g chopped almonds

Preparation instructions:
1. Preheat the Ninja Dual Zone Air Fryer to 160°C on zone 1 for 5 minutes.
2. In a bowl, whisk together the flour, granulated sugar, baking powder, and salt.
3. In another bowl, beat the eggs and almond extract until well combined.
4. Gradually add the egg mixture to the dry ingredients, stirring until a dough forms.
5. Fold in the chopped almonds.
6. On a lightly floured surface, shape the dough into a log, about 20 cm long and 5cm wide.
7. Place the log in zone 1 of the air fryer and cook at 160°C for 25 minutes or until golden brown and firm to the touch.
8. Once cooked, remove the almond biscotti from the air fryer and let it cool for a few minutes.
9. Transfer the biscotti to a cutting board and slice it diagonally into 1.5cm thick slices.
10. Place the biscotti slices back in the air fryer and cook at 160°C for an additional 5 minutes or until they are crisp and dry.
11. Once cooked, remove the biscotti from the air fryer and let them cool completely. Enjoy these crunchy almond biscotti with your favourite hot beverage.

Oreo Cheesecake Bites

Serves: 4
Prep time: 15 minutes / Cook time: 20 minutes

Ingredients:
- 150g Oreo cookies, crushed
- 40g unsalted butter, melted
- 200g cream cheese
- 80g powdered sugar
- 1 large egg
- 1/2 tsp vanilla extract
- Crushed Oreo cookies, for garnish

Preparation instructions:
1. Preheat the Ninja Dual Zone Air Fryer to 160°C on zone 1 for 5 minutes.
2. In a bowl, mix the crushed Oreo cookies and melted butter until well combined.
3. Line 4 cupcake moulds or silicone muffin cups with cupcake liners.
4. Divide the Oreo mixture among the cupcake liners, pressing it firmly into the bottom to form the crust.
5. In another bowl, beat the cream cheese, powdered sugar, egg, and vanilla extract until smooth and creamy.
6. Spoon the cream cheese mixture over the Oreo crust in each cupcake liner, filling them almost to the top.
7. Place the cupcake moulds or cups in zone 1 of the air fryer and cook at 160°C for 20 minutes or until the edges are set and the centres are slightly jiggly.
8. Once cooked, remove the Oreo cheesecake bites from the air fryer and let them cool in the moulds or cups for a few minutes.
9. Transfer the cheesecake bites to a wire rack to cool completely.
10. Before serving, garnish with crushed Oreo cookies. Enjoy these decadent and irresistible Oreo cheesecake bites as a delightful dessert or party treat.

Chapter 9: Staples, Sauces, Dips, and Dressings

Homemade Tater Tots

Serves: 4
Prep time: 15 minutes / Cook time: 20 minutes

Ingredients:
- 400g peeled and grated potatoes
- 1/2 small onion, finely chopped
- 2 tbsp all-purpose flour
- 1/2 tsp garlic powder
- 1/2 tsp onion powder
- 1/4 tsp paprika
- Salt and black pepper, to taste
- Vegetable oil, for spraying

Preparation instructions:
1. Preheat the Ninja Dual Zone Air Fryer to 200°C on zone 1 for 5 minutes.
2. In a bowl, combine the grated potatoes, chopped onion, all-purpose flour, garlic powder, onion powder, paprika, salt, and black pepper. Mix well.
3. Take a small portion of the mixture and shape it into a cylindrical tater tot.
4. Repeat the process until all the mixture is used, making approximately 16 tater tots.
5. Spray the tater tots with vegetable oil to help them crisp up.
6. Place the tater tots in zone 1 of the air fryer and cook at 200°C for 20 minutes or until golden brown and crispy, flipping them halfway through.
7. Once cooked, remove the tater tots from the air fryer and let them cool for a few minutes before serving. Enjoy these crispy and flavorful homemade tater tots as a delicious snack or side dish.

Roasted Red Pepper Hummus

Serves: 4
Prep time: 10 minutes / Cook time: 15 minutes

Ingredients:
- 2 large red bell peppers
- 240g canned chickpeas, rinsed and drained
- 2 cloves garlic
- 2 tbsp tahini
- 2 tbsp lemon juice
- 2 tbsp extra virgin olive oil
- 1/2 tsp ground cumin
- Salt and black pepper, to taste
- Fresh parsley, for garnish (optional)

Preparation instructions:
1. Preheat the Ninja Dual Zone Air Fryer to 200°C on zone 1 for 5 minutes.
2. Cut the red bell peppers in half, remove the seeds and stem, and place them in zone 1 of the air fryer.
3. Roast the bell peppers at 200°C for 15 minutes or until the skins are charred and blistered.
4. Once roasted, remove the bell peppers from the air fryer and let them cool for a few minutes.
5. Peel off the charred skins from the bell peppers and discard.
6. In a food processor, combine the roasted bell peppers, chickpeas, garlic, tahini, lemon juice, olive oil, ground cumin, salt, and black pepper.
7. Process the mixture until smooth and creamy, scraping down the sides as needed.
8. Taste and adjust the seasoning if necessary.
9. Transfer the roasted red pepper hummus to a serving bowl and garnish with fresh parsley if desired.
10. Serve with pita bread, vegetable sticks, or your favourite crackers. Enjoy this vibrant and flavorful roasted red pepper hummus as a tasty dip or spread.

Cilantro Lime Rice

Serves: 4
Prep time: 5 minutes / Cook time: 15 minutes

Ingredients:
- 200g basmati rice
- 400ml vegetable broth
- 30g fresh cilantro, chopped
- 2 tbsp lime juice
- Salt, to taste

Preparation instructions:
1. Rinse the basmati rice under cold water until the water runs clear.
2. In a saucepan, combine the rinsed rice and vegetable broth.
3. Bring the mixture to a boil over medium heat.
4. Reduce the heat to low, cover the saucepan, and let the rice simmer for 10-12 minutes or until the liquid is absorbed and the rice is cooked.
5. Remove the saucepan from the heat and let the rice sit, covered, for 5 minutes.
6. In a small bowl, mix together the chopped cilantro, lime juice, and salt.
7. Fluff the cooked rice with a fork, then drizzle the cilantro lime mixture over the rice.
8. Air fry at 175°C for 3 minutes.
9. Gently toss the rice to combine all the flavours.
10. Adjust the seasoning if needed.
11. Serve the cilantro lime rice as a refreshing and aromatic side dish to complement your favourite Mexican or Asian-inspired meals.

Hummus Dip With Veggie Crisps

Serves: 4
Prep time: 10 minutes / Cook time: 3 minutes

Ingredients:
- 240g canned chickpeas, rinsed and drained
- 2 cloves garlic
- 2 tbsp tahini
- 2 tbsp lemon juice
- 2 tbsp extra virgin olive oil
- 1/2 tsp ground cumin
- Salt and black pepper, to taste
- Assorted vegetable crisps, for serving

Preparation instructions:
1. In a food processor, combine the chickpeas, garlic, tahini, lemon juice, olive oil, ground cumin, salt, and black pepper.
2. Process the mixture until smooth and creamy, scraping down the sides as needed.
3. Taste and adjust the seasoning if necessary.
4. Air fry at 175°C for 3 minutes.
5. Transfer the hummus to a serving bowl.
6. Serve the hummus with an assortment of vegetable crisps, such as carrot sticks, cucumber slices, bell pepper strips, or celery sticks.
7. Enjoy this flavorful and nutritious hummus dip with veggie crisps as a wholesome snack or party appetisers.

Peanut Butter Oatmeal Bake

Serves: 4
Prep time: 10 minutes / Cook time: 20 minutes

Ingredients:
- 100g rolled oats
- 240 ml milk
- 60g peanut butter
- 2 tbsp honey
- 1/2 tsp vanilla extract
- 1/4 tsp cinnamon
- 1/4 tsp salt
- 30g chopped peanuts (optional)

Preparation instructions:
1. Preheat the Ninja Dual Zone Air Fryer to 180°C on zone 1 for 5 minutes.
2. In a mixing bowl, combine the rolled oats, milk, peanut butter, honey, vanilla extract, cinnamon, and salt. Mix well until all the

ingredients are evenly incorporated.
3. Pour the mixture into a greased oven-safe dish or silicone baking mould.
4. Sprinkle the chopped peanuts on top if desired.
5. Place the dish in zone 1 of the air fryer and bake at 180°C for 20 minutes or until the oatmeal bake is set and lightly golden on top.
6. Once cooked, remove from the air fryer and let it cool for a few minutes before serving. Serve warm and enjoy this delicious and nutritious peanut butter oatmeal bake for breakfast or as a wholesome snack.

Egg Fried Rice

Serves: 4
Prep time: 10 minutes / Cook time: 10 minutes

Ingredients:
- 300g cooked and cooled long-grain rice
- 2 large eggs, lightly beaten
- 60g frozen peas and carrots, thawed
- 1 small onion, finely chopped
- 2 cloves garlic, minced
- 2 tbsp soy sauce
- 1 tbsp sesame oil
- 2 spring onions, chopped (for garnish)
- Salt and black pepper, to taste

Preparation instructions:
1. Preheat the Ninja Dual Zone Air Fryer to 200°C on zone 1 for 5 minutes.
2. In a bowl, break up the cooked and cooled rice to separate any clumps.
3. In a separate bowl, beat the eggs and set aside.
4. Place the chopped onion and minced garlic in zone 1 of the air fryer and cook at 200°C for 3 minutes, stirring occasionally.
5. Add the thawed peas and carrots to the onion and garlic mixture and cook for an additional 2 minutes.
6. Push the vegetables to one side of the air fryer basket and pour the beaten eggs onto the other side.
7. Cook the eggs at 200°C for 1-2 minutes, stirring gently, until they are scrambled and fully cooked.
8. Combine the cooked rice with the vegetables and eggs in the air fryer basket.
9. Drizzle the soy sauce and sesame oil over the rice mixture. Season with salt and black pepper to taste.
10. Stir everything together, ensuring the rice is evenly coated with the seasonings and ingredients.
11. Cook at 200°C for another 3-4 minutes or until the fried rice is heated through.
12. Garnish with chopped spring onions and serve hot as a flavorful and satisfying main dish or side.

Honey Mustard Dressing

Makes: Approximately 180ml
Prep time: 5 minutes / Cook time: 3-4 minutes

Ingredients:
- 2 tbsp Dijon mustard
- 2 tbsp honey
- 2 tbsp apple cider vinegar
- 120ml extra virgin olive oil
- Salt and black pepper, to taste

Preparation instructions:
1. In a bowl, whisk together the Dijon mustard, honey, apple cider vinegar, salt, and black pepper.
2. Slowly drizzle in the olive oil while whisking continuously until the dressing emulsifies and thickens.
3. Taste and adjust the seasoning if needed.
4. Air fry at 180°C for 3-4 minutes.
5. Transfer the honey mustard dressing to a jar or bottle with a tight-fitting lid.
6. Store in the refrigerator for up to one week.
7. Shake well before using. This honey mustard dressing is perfect for salads, sandwiches, or as a delicious dipping sauce.

Tahini Sauce

Makes: Approximately 180ml
Prep time: 5 minutes / Cook time: 3-4 minutes

Ingredients:
- 120g tahini
- 60ml water
- 2 tbsp lemon juice
- 1 clove garlic, minced
- 1/4 tsp salt
- 1/4 tsp ground cumin

Preparation instructions:
1. In a bowl, whisk together the tahini, water, lemon juice, minced garlic, salt, and ground cumin.
2. Continue whisking until the ingredients are well combined and the sauce has a smooth consistency.
3. Taste and adjust the seasoning if necessary.
4. If the sauce is too thick, add more water, a tablespoon at a time, until desired consistency is reached.
5. Air fry at 180°C for 3-4 minutes.
6. Transfer the tahini sauce to a jar or bottle with a tight-fitting lid.
7. Store in the refrigerator for up to one week.
8. Stir well before using. This versatile tahini sauce can be used as a dip, salad dressing, or drizzled over roasted vegetables or grilled meats.

Baked Camembert With Croutons

Serves: 4
Prep time: 5 minutes / Cook time: 10 minutes

Ingredients:
- 1 round of Camembert cheese (about 250g)
- 4 slices of bread, cut into cubes
- 2 tbsp olive oil
- 2 cloves garlic, minced
- Fresh thyme leaves, for garnish
- Cranberry sauce, for serving (optional)

Preparation instructions:
1. Preheat the Ninja Dual Zone Air Fryer to 180°C on zone 1 for 5 minutes.
2. Place the Camembert cheese in a small oven-safe dish or silicone baking mould.
3. In a bowl, toss the bread cubes with olive oil and minced garlic until evenly coated.
4. Spread the bread cubes in zone 2 of the air fryer basket.
5. Place the Camembert dish and the air fryer basket with the bread cubes in the air fryer.
6. Bake at 180°C for 8-10 minutes or until the cheese is soft and gooey, and the bread cubes are golden and crispy.
7. Remove from the air fryer and let the baked Camembert and croutons cool for a few minutes.
8. Garnish the melted Camembert with fresh thyme leaves.
9. Serve with cranberry sauce on the side, if desired.
10. Enjoy this delightful and indulgent baked Camembert with crispy garlic croutons as a tasty appetiser or party snack.

Pesto Sauce

Makes: Approximately 180ml
Prep time: 10 minutes / Cook time: 3-4 minutes

Ingredients:
- 50g fresh basil leaves
- 30g pine nuts
- 30g grated Parmesan cheese
- 2 cloves garlic
- 120ml extra virgin olive oil
- Salt and black pepper, to taste

Preparation instructions:
1. In a food processor or blender, combine the fresh basil leaves, pine nuts, grated Parmesan cheese, and garlic.
2. Pulse the ingredients a few times to break them down.
3. While the food processor is running, slowly pour in the olive oil in a steady stream.
4. Continue blending until the pesto has a smooth and creamy consistency.

5. Taste and season with salt and black pepper as desired.
6. Air fry at 180°C for 3-4 minutes.
7. Transfer the pesto sauce to a jar or container with a tight-fitting lid.
8. Store in the refrigerator for up to one week.
9. Use this vibrant and aromatic pesto sauce to toss with pasta, spread on sandwiches, or as a flavorful addition to roasted vegetables or grilled meats.

Spicy Sriracha Mayo

Makes: Approximately 180ml
Prep time: 5 minutes / Cook time: 3-4 minutes

Ingredients:
- 120ml mayonnaise
- 2 tbsp Sriracha sauce
- 1 tbsp lime juice
- 1/2 tsp honey
- Salt, to taste

Preparation instructions:
1. In a bowl, whisk together the mayonnaise, Sriracha sauce, lime juice, honey, and salt.
2. Continue whisking until all the ingredients are well combined and the sauce is smooth.
3. Taste and adjust the seasoning according to your preference.
4. Air fry at 180°C for 3-4 minutes.
5. Transfer the spicy Sriracha mayo to a jar or bottle with a tight-fitting lid.
6. Store in the refrigerator for up to one week.
7. Stir well before using. This creamy and fiery sauce is perfect for adding a spicy kick to burgers, sandwiches, wraps, or as a dipping sauce for fries and appetisers.

Basil Aioli

Makes: Approximately 180ml
Prep time: 5 minutes / Cook time: 3-4 minutes

Ingredients:
- 2 cloves garlic, minced
- 120ml mayonnaise
- 1 tbsp fresh basil leaves, finely chopped
- 1 tbsp lemon juice
- Salt and black pepper, to taste

Preparation instructions:
1. In a bowl, combine the minced garlic, mayonnaise, chopped basil leaves, and lemon juice.
2. Stir well until all the ingredients are thoroughly mixed.
3. Season with salt and black pepper to taste.
4. Air fry at 180°C for 3-4 minutes.
5. Transfer the basil aioli to a jar or container with a tight-fitting lid.
6. Refrigerate for at least 30 minutes to allow the flavours to meld together.
7. Serve as a delicious dip for fries, spread on sandwiches, or as a flavorful accompaniment to grilled meats and roasted vegetables.

Harissa Sauce

Makes: Approximately 180ml
Prep time: 10 minutes / Cook time: 3-4 minutes

Ingredients:
- 3 tbsp harissa paste
- 2 tbsp olive oil
- 1 tbsp lemon juice
- 1 clove garlic, minced
- 1/4 tsp ground cumin
- Salt, to taste

Preparation instructions:
1. In a bowl, whisk together the harissa paste, olive oil, lemon juice, minced garlic, ground cumin, and salt.
2. Continue whisking until all the ingredients are well combined and the sauce has a smooth consistency.
3. Taste and adjust the seasoning if needed.
4. Air fry at 180°C for 3-4 minutes.

5. Transfer the harissa sauce to a jar or container with a tight-fitting lid.
6. Refrigerate for at least 30 minutes to allow the flavours to develop.
7. Use this vibrant and spicy harissa sauce to add a fiery kick to roasted vegetables, grilled meats, or as a flavorful condiment for sandwiches and wraps.

Chinese Dumpling Sauce

Makes: Approximately 180ml
Prep time: 5 minutes / Cook time: 3-4 minutes

Ingredients:
- 3 tbsp soy sauce
- 2 tbsp rice vinegar
- 1 tbsp sesame oil
- 1 tbsp honey or brown sugar
- 1 clove garlic, minced
- 1/2 tsp grated ginger
- 1/4 tsp chilli flakes (optional)

Preparation instructions:
1. In a bowl, whisk together the soy sauce, rice vinegar, sesame oil, honey or brown sugar, minced garlic, grated ginger, and chilli flakes (if using).
2. Continue whisking until all the ingredients are well combined.
3. Taste and adjust the sweetness or spiciness according to your preference.
4. Air fry at 180°C for 3-4 minutes.
5. Transfer the Chinese dumpling sauce to a jar or container with a tight-fitting lid.
6. Refrigerate for at least 30 minutes to allow the flavours to meld together.
7. Serve as a dipping sauce for dumplings, potstickers, or spring rolls, or use as a flavorful marinade for meats and vegetables.

Creamy Avocado Dressing

Makes: Approximately 180ml
Prep time: 5 minutes / Cook time: 3-4 minutes

Ingredients:
- 1 ripe avocado
- 2 tbsp Greek yoghurt
- 2 tbsp lime juice
- 60ml olive oil
- 1 clove garlic, minced
- 1/4 tsp ground cumin
- Salt and black pepper, to taste

Preparation instructions:
1. In a blender or food processor, combine the ripe avocado, Greek yoghurt, lime juice, olive oil, minced garlic, ground cumin, salt, and black pepper.
2. Blend until the ingredients are well combined and the dressing has a smooth and creamy texture.
3. Taste and adjust the seasoning if needed.
4. Air fry at 180°C for 3-4 minutes.
5. Transfer the creamy avocado dressing to a jar or container with a tight-fitting lid.
6. Refrigerate for at least 30 minutes to allow the flavours to develop.
7. Drizzle this luscious dressing over salads, use as a dip for vegetables, or as a flavorful topping for tacos and grilled meats.

Basil Walnut Pesto

Makes: Approximately 180ml
Prep time: 10 minutes / Cook time: 3-4 minutes

Ingredients:
- 240g fresh basil leaves
- 70g walnuts
- 2 cloves garlic
- 120ml olive oil
- 50g grated Parmesan cheese
- Salt and black pepper, to taste

Preparation instructions:
1. In a blender or food processor, combine the fresh basil leaves, walnuts, garlic cloves, olive oil, grated Parmesan cheese, salt, and black pepper.
2. Blend until all the ingredients are well incorporated and the pesto has a smooth consistency.

3. Taste and adjust the seasoning if needed.
4. Air fry at 180°C for 3-4 minutes.
5. Transfer the basil walnut pesto to a jar or container with a tight-fitting lid.
6. Refrigerate for at least 30 minutes to allow the flavours to meld together.
7. Use this aromatic and nutty pesto as a sauce for pasta, spread on sandwiches, or as a flavorful addition to roasted vegetables and grilled meats.

Coconut Curry Sauce

Makes: Approximately 180ml
Prep time: 10 minutes / Cook time: 6-8 minutes

Ingredients:
- 1 can (400ml) coconut milk
- 2 tbsp curry powder
- 2 tbsp soy sauce
- 1 tbsp lime juice
- 1 tbsp brown sugar
- 1 clove garlic, minced
- 1/2 tsp grated ginger
- Salt, to taste

Preparation instructions:
1. In a saucepan, combine the coconut milk, curry powder, soy sauce, lime juice, brown sugar, minced garlic, grated ginger, and salt.
2. Place the saucepan over medium heat and bring the mixture to a gentle simmer.
3. Stir occasionally and let it simmer for about 5 minutes to allow the flavours to meld together.
4. Taste and adjust the seasoning if needed.
5. Air fry at 180°C for 3-4 minutes.
6. Let the coconut curry sauce cool.
7. Transfer to a jar or container with a tight-fitting lid.
8. Refrigerate until ready to use.
9. This creamy and fragrant coconut curry sauce is perfect for serving with rice, dipping spring rolls, or as a flavorful topping for grilled chicken or seafood.

Refried Bean Dip

Serves: 4-6
Prep time: 10 minutes / Cook time: 10 minutes

Ingredients:
- 400g canned pinto beans, drained and rinsed
- 1 tbsp olive oil
- 1 small onion, diced
- 1 clove garlic, minced
- 1/2 tsp ground cumin
- 1/4 tsp chilli powder
- Salt, to taste
- 60ml water
- Fresh cilantro, chopped (for garnish, optional)

Preparation instructions:
1. In a saucepan, heat the olive oil over medium heat.
2. Add the diced onion and minced garlic to the pan and sauté until the onion is translucent.
3. Stir in the ground cumin and chilli powder, and cook for an additional minute to toast the spices.
4. Add the pinto beans to the pan and season with salt.
5. Pour in the water and bring the mixture to a simmer.
6. Reduce the heat to low and let the beans simmer for about 5 minutes, allowing the flavours to meld together.
7. Use a potato masher or fork to mash the beans until you reach your desired consistency.
8. If the dip is too thick, add a splash of water and continue mashing until smooth.
9. Taste and adjust the seasoning if needed.
10. Remove from heat and transfer the refried bean dip to a serving bowl.
11. Garnish with fresh chopped cilantro, if desired.
12. Serve warm with tortilla chips or as a delicious filling for quesadillas and burritos.
13. Note: The Ninja Dual Zone Air Fryer can be used to reheat the refried bean dip before serving. Simply place the dip in a heat-safe dish and warm it in the air fryer at 180°C for a few minutes until heated through.

Printed in Great Britain
by Amazon